Critical Guides to French Texts

Critical Guides to French Texts

EDITED BY ROGER LITTLE, WOLFGANG VAN EMDEN, DAVID WILLIAMS

SIMON

Histoire

Anthony Cheal Pugh

Lecturer in French,
University of Durham

Grant & Cutler Ltd
1982

©   Grant & Cutler Ltd
      1982
ISBN 0 7293 0143 5

I.S.B.N. 84-499-6040-1

DEPÓSITO LEGAL: V. 2.707 - 1982

Printed in Spain by
Artes Gráficas Soler, S.A., Valencia
for
GRANT & CUTLER LTD
11 BUCKINGHAM STREET, LONDON W.C.2

Contents

Prefatory Note

This 'Critical Guide' to Claude Simon's *Histoire* does not set out to provide a comprehensive survey of existing criticism relating to the novel. Little has in fact appeared in the way of detailed analysis of the work's themes and structure, and *Histoire* is too long and too complex for the task to be undertaken in a short treatment such as this.

Instead, I have tried to focus upon what I consider to be some central issues, many of which arise out of the initial question of *how to read* a text that may well appear to be formless and chaotic. I hope to have shown some of the ways in which the writing itself can direct our exploration of the welter of images that compose the novel, by means of patterns of repetition and transformation.

What follows is thus more a series of forays into the dense verbal material of *Histoire*, than a synoptic view of this rich and enigmatic novel. As a consequence, large areas of the 'story' (such as the Spanish episode) are left by the wayside. I accept full responsibility for these and any other omissions, since my purpose was to engage the text in depth, not in the hope that it would give up its secrets, but because the novel's power to fascinate lies in the centrality of questions involving absence, desire, transgression, memory and representation, questions which critics such as Roland Barthes have seen to lie at the heart of literature itself:

> la littérature la plus 'vraie', c'est celle qui se sait la plus irréelle, dans la mesure où elle se sait essentiellement langage, c'est cette recherche d'un état intermédiaire aux choses et aux mots, c'est cette tension d'une conscience qui est à la fois portée et limitée par les mots, qui dispose à travers eux d'un pouvoir *à la fois absolu et improbable.*
> (Roland Barthes, *Essais critiques*)

Page numbers in brackets refer to the Gallimard ('Folio') edition of *Histoire*. Other references, in the style (*2*, p.66), refer to the numbered critical texts in the Bibliography.

Since there is no index to the twelve sections of the novel, the following references may be found useful:

I	11-42
II	43-75
III	76-108
IV	109-147
V	148-184
VI	185-221
VII	222-242
VIII	243-287
IX	288-307
X	308-346
XI	347-386
XII	387-435

Durham   A.C.P.

1. Introduction and Background

'le monde est fait de telle sorte qu'il ne
puisse être exprimé que dans des
'histoires' et comme montré du doigt'
(Merleau-Ponty)

I Fiction and truth

Histoire is a novel which confronts the reader with the age-old
paradox summed up by Stendhal when he declared that art is 'un
beau mensonge', for it asks, once again, how fiction can relate
to truth, and 'stories' to 'history'. In so doing, the novel poses a
number of philosophical, psychological and aesthetic problems
which I shall attempt to explain in this 'critical guide'.

In spite of the considerable critical reputation that *Histoire*
enjoys, very little detailed analysis of the text has so far appeared, and few critics have tackled what I consider to be a central issue, namely the presence, behind the fiction, of a strong
autobiographical element. What is at stake here is, however, not
so much what may or may not have happened to Claude Simon
at crucial moments in his life, but the ways in which readers will
react to a text. On the one hand there are the deeply personal
memories of a writer, and on the other a published text —
something literally 'made public'. The critic and the reader have
access only to printed words on paper, and what has been called
the 'existential gap' between writer and reader is bridged only by
linguistic signs.

The relationship between writer, text, and reader is a subject
which is today receiving a degree of attention, from literary
theorists, which is unprecedented. It is as if we were suddenly
unsure of what actually happens when we read. Are we just in a
world of illusion or fantasy when we read a novel, convinced
merely by belief or convention that the world depicted is a copy

of the real one? Can novels provide instructive models of real experience? Are the emotions produced in us while we read genuine, or spurious? *Histoire* asks all these questions, directly or indirectly, and shows how particularly suggestive and ambiguous works can *anticipate* the theoretical discussions of critics, or how, to put it another way, the practice of writing, when pursued by writers of integrity, is itself a critical activity.

Since my claim is that *Histoire*'s great emotional power is related to biographical sources, it might be thought that I am being deluded by what has been called 'the genetic fallacy', or the attempt to reconstruct the author from the fictional text and bridge the so-called 'existential gap'. What I shall be seeking to demonstrate is not, however, that the novel reproduces episodes from its author's life, nor, indeed, that it is in any way a truthful account of such episodes. The kind of truth that I shall be discussing may in fact be a myth, for it is by definition inaccessible, locked away in the writer's memory, perhaps literally buried in the past. Memories can only be evoked in words, and in the present, and these words, even if they are the vehicle for the writer's feelings, can only produce in the reader echoes and traces of their origin: if we have learned anything at all from twentieth-century linguistics, it is that words are merely signs that function in relation to other signs. Any description of what is 'communicated' by a literary work must cope with this fact; the reader will always remain at a distance from the author's experience. What we probably mean, therefore, when we describe a work as 'authentic', is that it has produced in us echoes of our own experience. I shall try to show how *Histoire* achieves precisely that, by dealing with a number of 'universal' themes and events which, by their very banality, create an effect of resonance in readers.

II The writer: artist or artisan?

The discretion of Simon's critics regarding the biographical sources of *Histoire* is basically a response to the writer's own natural modesty: Claude Simon is not given to self-exhibition, and rather than talk about himself he will usually prefer to talk about the progress of his work and the problems which face him as he puts together the pieces of another novel. In the numerous interviews that he has given, and in the conversations that I have had with him since 1969, when I first went to see him in Paris, what has impressed me most of all has been his exceptional artistic honesty. His love of painting is well known, as is his description of himself as 'un peintre raté'. He is clearly unfair to himself, but his preoccupation with the visual, and with the problems involved in artistic representation in general has long been noted.

Frequently, Simon refers to his work as that of a craftsman, patiently assembling the components that will make up the finished work. Using a telling image, he once described his writings as comparable to the work of an artisan, producing 'repoussé' designs on a sheet of copper, designs which are made from behind the metal, their effect invisible to the artisan himself. At other times he has used the term 'bricolage' in order to indicate the element of chance in his work, and his tendency to use whatever material is at hand. He calls the results 'collages' because of the way he incorporates ready-made written material into his novels, and because his method of composition involves rearranging fragments of texts, written sometimes over a long period, into a final shape determined more by formal criteria derived from painting than by what he considers to be the debased, if not absurd logic of traditional fiction (see *3*, pp.74-8). The reliance upon chronological sequence is, for Simon, an abdication of the writer's responsibility to the truth of his own experience, and life, he stresses, is not ordered in the ways implied by conventional novels. Events do not occur in 'logical' ways, and perception itself is a chaos of remembrance, imagining, and awareness of present sensations.

III Realism

The present-day reader's attitude towards fiction has necessarily been conditioned, to a greater or to a lesser extent, by the achievements of nineteenth-century realism. There is, as Jean Ricardou observes (*13*, p.28), a realist lurking in all of us,

and even when we read works whose authors have expressly re-
jected realist criteria, as the 'new novelists' have done, we still
tend to imagine that what the fiction describes has an
autonomous existence, beyond or behind the printed page. The
'materialist' philosophy of writing, which has emerged from the
'new novel' movement, and which was already influencing
Claude Simon as he wrote *Histoire*, involves a new attitude
towards reading, some of the implications of which I shall be ex-
amining. For the moment, however, it is important to note that
as late as 1960 Simon described himself as 'un réaliste total' (he
was talking about *La Route des Flandres*).[1] What Simon meant
by the term 'réaliste' was, quite simply, that what he tried to do
while writing was to describe, as accurately as possible, the
workings of his own mind, as his memory and his imagination
combined in the production of a fiction. The task that he set
himself was thus similar to that undertaken by 'phenomenological' philosophers, such as Husserl, the early Sartre,
and Merleau-Ponty.

Maurice Merleau-Ponty held the chair of philosophy at the
Collège de France between 1952 and 1961, and was so impressed
by Simon's novels (particularly *La Route des Flandres*) that he
used examples from them in his lectures, in order to make points
about perception, self-awareness, and the ways in which we
mentally and physically inhabit the spatial and temporal dimensions.

The type of 'realism' that is to be found in Simon's novels between 1957 and 1967 (or the 'second period') has thus been
described as 'phenomenological', since it involves essentially
subjective descriptions of how we perceive ourselves in relation
to phenomena. While *Histoire* is open to critical readings based
upon the notion of 'phenomenological realism' it is my opinion
that such readings are valid only as an initial strategy for ap-
proaching the novel. It can be shown, for example that while
Histoire appears to be narrated from the fixed point of view of
the first person narrator, the whole question of the 'identity' of
both the narrator and some of the characters in the novel is

---

[1] In an interview with H. Juin: 'Les secrets d'un romancier', *Les Lettres
Françaises*, no. 844, 6-12 octobre 1960, p.5.

made problematic by the writing itself (see Chapter 3). Similarly, although the action of the novel is 'framed' within a twenty-four hour period in the fictional present, the past invades, and even overwhelms the present, threatening the apparent chronological structure of the narrative: the reader finds that the basically realist outer 'frame' can no longer contain the proliferating fragments of the text. Ultimately, he finds himself obliged to reassemble the pieces in a new, but probably temporary order, which will itself have to be replaced, in each successive reading, as new pathways through the text are opened up, and new connections recognised. What was a passive 'realist' reading is transformed, by the writing, into a creative act.

IV History

The reader's access to the claustrophobic subjective world of *Histoire* is made easier by the descriptions of postcards and photographs which punctuate the text, for in many cases the scenes depicted are familiar ones — the reader can thus supply similar images from his memory, perhaps even memories of some of the same images described by the writer. This feature of the novel thus introduces into the text a significant dimension of collective experience, and above all a sense of a common historical past, nowhere more graphically expressed than in the following description of a war-torn landscape:

> et encore cette photographie d'un champ de bataille prise d'avion (pas la terre, le damier des prés, des labours, des bois: une étendue croûteuse, pustuleuse, comme une maladie du sol même, une lèpre, sous l'effet de laquelle les reliefs, les ravins, les tracés rectilignes des anciennes constructions auraient été pour ainsi dire gommés ou plutôt déglutis, attaqués par quelque acide, quelque suintement purulent) et qui illustrait une des dernières pages du manuel d'Histoire, comme si celle-ci (l'Histoire) s'arrêtait là (pp.115-16)

The photograph in question, it later appears, illustrates the aftermath of the battle of Verdun, but for today's readers it may seem to depict equally well the scene which would confront any survivors of a nuclear war. What appeared to Simon's narrator as a child to be the 'last page' in our history could apply just as well to us. The point that I am making here is that our response to a work of art will depend very much upon two things, firstly the generalising potential of the images used and secondly our own horizon of expectation in the present. However much we project imaginatively into the past, what we see or read has an effect and a value which are essentially dependent upon our present situation. The example of the photograph serves also to remind us that photography has totally altered our perception of the past, and thus our attitude towards history.

The peculiar power of photographs lies in the elimination of historical distance that they can achieve. An event, frozen in time, persists into the present, collapsing the protective barrier of temporal perspective, and abolishing the screen of amnesia which allows the memory to function — for as Samuel Beckett said of Proust, if we could not forget anything, we would not be able to remember anything. Claude Simon is acutely aware of the modification of our awareness of time brought about by photography and film, making frequent use of allusions to both still-photography and cinema in his novel. If one of the aims of art is to renew our perception of ourselves and our world, then Simon's work can certainly help us to process and interpret the welter of images that assail us daily.

Much of sections IX and X of *Histoire* is devoted to the description of a photograph (see Chapter 7), this time of a group of people in a painter's studio. As we shall see, much of what the novel has to tell us about history, truth and fiction centres upon the question of representation, whether it be in photography, in painting, or in language. In a novel, whose elements are linguistic, and exclusively so, all representations, and all images, pass through words. The conventions of realism have tended to allow us to forget this. Claude Simon, like the novelists he most admires, Flaubert, Proust, Joyce and Faulkner, sees how language conditions and limits our experience, and how it must be adapted, stretched if necessary, before it can begin to provide adequate accounts of how we respond to reality. *Histoire* takes us to the limits of psychological realism, to the point where we have to re-examine the way in which we see ourselves in relation to the past.

The past is seen, in all Simon's novels of the first and second 'periods', in a dual perspective: there is the past of family and personal relationships (a web of 'histoires' in the sense of a complex mixture of legend, scandal and hearsay), and there is the collective past of European civilisation, what Simon's narrator refers to as '*l'Histoire*', with the ironic capital H.

Using the stark background of the 'Great War', the Russian revolution, the Spanish civil war, and the second world war (all of which indelibly marked his childhood, youth and early manhood) Simon's novels can be seen to represent, at many levels, an attempt to come to grips with our peculiarly Western obsession with history, for they show how, out of the philosophical and economic optimism of the eighteenth century, has come a manichean world of diametrically opposed values. Simon's preoccupation with history, with art, and with death has led to comparisons with André Malraux, but there are no heroics in Simon's novels, no 'fraternité virile' to compensate for the awareness of death and the absence of salvation. Nor is 'the Absurd' set up as the source of alternative values: Simon's characters are in revolt, but fail ultimately in their various attempts to escape from the pressures of history. Instead, in a state of almost paralysed detachment, they observe in themselves and their fellows, ironic and repetitive patterns of hope and despair, becoming ever more aware, in the process, of the passage of time and the fragility of the human condition.

V The novels of the 'second period'

The four novels of the 'second period', *L'Herbe* (1958), *La Route des Flandres* (1960), *Le Palace* (1962) and *Histoire* (1967) are linked, and can be read in sequence, although this does present a number of problems, which arise from Simon's attempt, in each successive novel, to break new ground in terms of both form and content:

mes livres sortent les uns des autres comme des tables
gigognes. Je n'aurais pas pu écrire *Histoire* sans avoir écrit
Le Palace, ni *Le Palace* sans *La Route des Flandres*. En
général, c'est avec ce qui n'a pu être dit dans un des livres
précédents que je commence un nouveau roman.[2]

Although *La Route des Flandres* is the second novel in the
group, it deals with a period prior to the one depicted in
L'Herbe, and its narrator 'Georges' is a secondary, and only
briefly perceived character in the earlier novel, which is narrated
from the point of view of his wife Louise. *L'Herbe*, for this and
other reasons, is thus marginal to the remaining three novels, a
prelude to them, written while Simon was still struggling to find
a way to write the story which appears in *La Route des Flandres*,
and which, he says, it took him twenty years to find. Once this
novel was written he was able to go back, beyond the setting of
the second world war, to the Spanish civil war (which had
already provided some of the material for an earlier novel, *Le
Sacre du printemps* (1954)) and write *Le Palace*. When this was
finished the journey back into the past could be completed, in
Histoire, which of course includes many scenes from the narrator's childhood. In each case, however, the leap-frogging
move back into the past is accompanied by a more or less symmetrical movement into the present, until in *Histoire* an almost
continuous temporal perspective is achieved.

The novels of the 'second period' are adequately summarised
in the various books on Claude Simon that are now available
(see *7, 9, 17*), and it suffices, for present purposes, to stress that
in spite of considerable formal differences between them, the
four works are closely related at the thematic level. Dominant
among their themes are love, war, passing time and death, and it
is in *Histoire* that they are most powerfully orchestrated and
unified.

Simon readily admits that death has been one of his constant
preoccupations. His father, whom he never knew, was killed
during the first world war, and he lost his mother while he was

---

[2] Claude Simon, quoted by T. de Saint-Phalle in 'Claude Simon, franc-tireur de
la révolution romanesque', *Le Figaro Littéraire*, 6 avril 1967.

still a child. In Barcelona, in 1936, he found himself involved in the chaos and violence of a revolution taking place within the context of a civil war, and in 1940, as a cavalryman, he narrowly escaped death on several occasions, during the *débâcle* that is described in *La Route des Flandres*. During the 1950s he witnessed the slow and agonising death, from cancer, of the uncle who had brought him up after the death of his father, and subsequently, Simon himself nearly died from a serious illness. Much of this background is alluded to in the early text entitled *La Corde raide* (1947), which was described by its publishers as 'souvenirs', but which is also an experiment in narrative technique, and an important, if sometimes over-emphatic statement of views on life and on art.

We do not in fact need such information in order to respond to *Histoire*, for the novel is concerned with universal human feelings, and that most universal of human experiences which is the death of loved ones. Such a theme has a 'generalising potential' which is self-evident.

Before looking in any detail at *Histoire* we must look for a moment at the two novels which precede it, and consider the question of the identities of their respective narrators in relation to the narrator of *Histoire*, for readers of the four novels frequently assume that the same person is involved.

The anonymous narrator of *Histoire* cannot however be identified wholly with the 'Georges' of *La Route des Flandres*, let alone the shadowy character who bears the same name in *L'Herbe*. In *Le Palace* the narrator is split into past and present incarnations, and the novel is more obviously complementary to *Histoire* than the two preceding ones. A considerable section of *Histoire* seems in fact to grow directly out of *Le Palace*, expanding some scenes of street-fighting during the anarchist insurrection in Barcelona in 1936. There is insufficient space in this study to examine in detail the links between the novels, or to go into the question of their complementarity. We should however note that the reappearance of certain names, from one novel to another, does not constitute the equivalent of a 'retour des personnages', and that we would be faced with unavoidable inconsistencies if we insisted upon treating the fictional worlds of the four novels as homogeneous.

For present purposes, I shall therefore treat *Histoire* as a self-contained novel, but one that brings with it a 'memory' of previous ones. As we shall see when we look more at Simon's view of the writing process, the names and scenes which link *Histoire* to the other novels of the 'second period' are transformed by the new text. Thus, although Claude Simon clearly uses personal memories in his writings, his creative practice does not allow us to imagine that his characters inhabit an unchanging landscape.

The 'intertextual' dimension of Simon's novels during the 'second period' has been studied by Gérard Roubichou in his book on *L'Herbe* (*15*). His conclusion is that the links between the novels are to be considered as more significant at a formal level than at the level of fictional content: the names and events which recur are thus best seen as 'motifs à variables' (*15*, p.25), rather than as stable elements:

> une parenté d'écriture lie toutes ces œuvres les unes aux autres, comme si d'un roman à l'autre se poursuivait, avec des composantes de plus en plus complexes, un 'même' texte marqué par une certaine continuité et obéissant à des lois ou à des mécanismes internes de prolifération.
>
> (*15*, pp.26-27)

As Roubichou observes here, Simon's novels could well be studied as if they were a continuous text, but each work nevertheless reveals a degree of formal unity which arises from a specific compositional logic, and this is determined by certain 'mécanismes internes de prolifération', that is, generative and associative patterns of words and images. We shall see how this applies to *Histoire* in Chapers 3 and 4, but before this we must look at the overall form of the novel.

2. The Form of the Novel

The outer 'frame' of the action in *Histoire* seems to cover a period of twenty-four hours, although this is not evident until the reader has reached the end of the novel. Initially, in the absence of numbered chapters, or even chapter headings, the reader is unable to project or predict any shape or pattern which might guide him. (See my prefatory note for page references to the twelve sections of the novel.) He is obliged, therefore, to plunge into the text, and sink or swim in the flow of the narration, which, in the first pages, has a particularly mesmerising quality, as the mysterious voices of the old ladies, like decrepit sirens, lure him into the labyrinth of the narrator's past.

Eventually, it becomes clear that the novel describes a continuous sequence of events in the present. In themselves they are unremarkable: the narrator awakens, gets up and washes, and goes to the bank, meeting on the way an old family acquaintance. At the bank he arranges a loan, after which he has lunch in a restaurant, and returns to the house. Here he meets an antique dealer to whom he sells the chest of drawers in which he has discovered the postcards sent by his father to his mother during the period of their engagement and the first years of their marriage. Among the postcards he finds a photograph in which he recognises his uncle Charles as a young man, posing with a group including a painter and a naked model in a Parisian studio. The narrator examines the photograph in great detail, speculating about the circumstances in which it was taken, and seems, for a while, to project himself into it, taking the place of his uncle. The confusion of identities which occurs here persists until the end of the novel, but the remainder of the narrator's activities are not difficult to follow: he tries (unsuccessfully) to contact his cousin Paulou by telephone, since he needs his signature on a document relating to the mortgage on the family property that he has arranged to order to secure the loan

negotiated earlier at the bank. In the late afternoon he drives to
Paulou's villa by the coast, returning to the city as night falls.
He goes out to a café during the evening, and as he returns home
watches his former friend Lambert, now an ambitious politi-
cian, emerging from an electoral meeting. Finally, alone again in
the deserted family house, he lies awake late into the night, as
the memories stimulated by the day's events surge up again, in
an increasingly fragmented and incoherent way.

Summarised in this way, the novel appears deceptively simple,
and in this chapter, I want to show how, in successive readings,
all our assumptions about its overall form become progressively
more tenuous.

What I call the 'overture' (or the first thirty pages) of *Histoire*
can seem, for example, to constitute an anticipation of the
novel's ending, after which, at the beginning of section II, we
return to the moment of the narrator's awakening. If this were
so, the period of time involved would be situated *after* the day's
events, and sections II to XII would consist, logically speaking,
of an enormous 'flashback'. There are various reasons for this
being an unsatisfactory interpretation, among them the fact that
the narrator refers to a *continuous* period of time, not a single
occasion:

> et l'été quand je travaillais tard dans la nuit assis devant la
> fenêtre ouverte je pouvais la voir (p.11)

During the 1971 colloquium on the *nouveau roman* (3),
Claude Simon used a diagram to illustrate the composition of
Histoire, and described it as follows:

> ...la composition d'*Histoire* pourrait être schématisée sous
> la forme de plusieurs sinusoïdes de longueur d'ondes
> variables qui courent tantôt au-dessus, tantôt au-dessous
> (invisibles alors) d'une ligne continue A A', apparaissant,
> disparaissant, se confondant, se coupant, interférant ou se
> séparant, la ligne étant en réalité une courbe de très grand
> rayon, un cercle qui revient à son point de départ (le nar-
> rateur étendu sur son lit) cependant que les périodes

d'oscillation des diverses sinusoïdes raccourcissent de plus
en plus, leurs crêtes alternant et se succédant à un rythme
de plus en plus précipité. (*3*, p.94)

Most critics accept that the novel is 'circular' in the way that
Simon describes, but as I have pointed out, the 'point de départ'
is not 'le narrateur étendu sur son lit', but the narrator sitting at
an open window. Simon was clearly referring to the beginning of
section II, and not to the 'overture'. The reason for this inac-
curacy is fairly simple: Simon described the novel as 'circular',
and drew his diagram, *after* the novel was written. In the question and answer session after his paper he confirmed this point
to me.

The diagram is thus a simplification, and suggests a formal
model for the text which is useful, but does not explain the gap
between the ending and the beginning of section II. We must
conclude, I think, that it is outside the chronological frame of
the main narrative, because it refers not to a particular evening,
but to the many evenings when the writer worked at his text. It
could therefore be said that the first section of the novel is
another 'frame', linking the fiction to the circumstances of its
production, and then dissolving once the narrator is awakened
by the birds, at the beginning of section II (p.43).

The only serious attempts to analyse the structure of *Histoire*
that have been so far made are a short and somewhat tentative
article by Gérard Roubichou (*16*), and a chapter on *Histoire* in
Les Romans de Claude Simon, by Stuart Sykes (*17*, pp.102-25),
which follows up Roubichou's analyses, but comes to different
conclusions.

Roubichou looks at the typographical composition of
Histoire, as well as the overall structure. He concludes that the
'*alinéas*', or paragraphs, or 'blocs' which make up the text, and
are its most distinctive feature, have the function of emphasising
discontinuity. Frequently, sentences are interrupted by *alinéas*,
in such a way that the basic syntactic unit, the sentence, already
threatened in Simon's work by sheer length, and the constant in-
terruption of parentheses, is threatened with dissolution:

> Signe de clarté dans l'académisme grammatical, l'alinéa
> devient dans *Histoire* signe de perturbation, instrument
> disjoncteur du discours, *brise-phrase*. (*16*, p.127)

In spite of this, says Roubichou, there is continuity in the syntax, for without it, the text would be unreadable. The disjunctive effect is thus frequently typographical only, producing a tension between the continuity we expect in narrative, and the discontinuity of experience which is concealed by conventional syntax and punctuation. Roubichou concludes that:

> Le texte d'*Histoire* invite, enfin, le lecteur à une lecture très
> active: au texte qui se livre entièrement émietté doit aussi
> correspondre un effort de recomposition. La linéarité, qui
> semble d'ordinaire aller de soi, devient tout á coup le lieu
> d'une mise en cause; car le jeu des alinéas successifs sup-
> pose une autre lecture en profondeur. Contester la linéarité
> tout en l'assumant, tel est un des caractères d'*Histoire*.
> (*16*, p.135)

Stuart Sykes, on the other hand, sees the themes of continuity and discontinuity as related, still, to Simon's desire to reproduce the quality of perception itself, of memory and sensation, both past and present, brought together in the act of writing: 'Ce n'est pas le drame d'action remémorée que cherche Claude Simon, mais celui de la mémoire elle-même et de son réveil sous la plume' (*17*, p.121). Disorder and discontinuity are inherent in perception itself, as the mind switches from one mode of apprehension to another, and Sykes illustrates this basically phenomenological approach by showing how paragraph transitions shift the text from past to present, and from one type of sense experience to another: 'La multiplicité de la perception se fragmente aussi pour créer les blocs textuels dont Simon se sert dans *Histoire* comme jamais auparavant' (*17*, p.117). The result, in Sykes's words, is 'le maintien d'un désordre positif' (*17*, p.118), and he summarises the writer's artistic aims in the following way:

> Alors, ce qui n'était que désordre devient clair: l'ordre recherché par Simon tente de traduire fidèlement et matériellement le processus par quoi mots et images s'agglutinent pour former une réalité toute subjective et mouvante. (*17*, p.121)

While agreeing with most of what Sykes advances, and with his conclusion, namely that '*Histoire* est à la fois l'un des ouvrages les plus expérimentaux de Claude Simon et un roman d'où se dégage cette nostalgie du temps passant que seule la grande littérature nous apporte' (*17*, pp.124-25), I feel that his remarks on *Histoire* do not give sufficient emphasis to the many ways in which the writer's work on language alters the nature of the raw material of the fiction (which may indeed be originally perceptual and sensory) and produces a new linguistic order which is frequently on the point of *taking over* from the one originally intended to translate the working of memory. Sykes is right to stress that it is the act of writing which activates the process, but I think that we shall see that the novel eventually obliges us to redefine the term 'memory' itself, in textual terms.

We should look, at this point, at part of a philosophical discussion of the workings of the memory:

> ... it is misleading to speak of remembering as though it involved a copy or a replica of a past scene. It is misleading because a copy or a replica should in fact resemble, to the point of complete likeness, the thing copied, whereas a memory in some sense always tends to remain unlike the remembered scene in that it will contain some things that were not the case and fail to contain others that were the case... I suggest therefore that genuine memories necessarily differ... from the original events to be remembered; that they display delusive features as the result of a certain creative imagination that we exercise in conjunction with remembering.[3]

---

[3] W. Von Leyden, *Remembering, A Philosophical Problem*, London, Duckworth, 1960, pp.84-85.

This could well apply to what happens in *Histoire*, where the creativity of the memory itself is doubled by the writer's activity. His work on language, and the subsequent process of composition — ordering, arranging, and rewriting the fragments of text — produce a verbal patchwork which no longer obeys the same laws as a linear narrative, where chronological succession allows only two temporal dimensions, the present and the past. We are free to read *Histoire* in this way, but once only, for on a second and successive readings, connections are established between images and metaphors which, if we were applying realist criteria, would suggest that the narrator was anticipating thoughts that occur to him *later on* in the period covered by the outer frame of the narrative. It thus becomes increasingly difficult to sustain the view that the text 'represents' the working of the narrator's memory: how could he know what his thoughts were going to be later on in the day? The shift that has occurred may appear to be a simple and obvious one: it is the reader who anticipates, and makes the connections. This is of course true, but only up to a point, for no reader could ever transfer the whole content of the novel to his own memory. The only objective structure available remains the text itself. Thus whereas the only 'real' memory involved in reading is clearly that of the reader himself, the text provides the only evidence that we can use if we are to say anything at all meaningful about the way the novel functions. Consequently, for the purpose of interpreting *Histoire*, we need a concept of memory which allows us to distinguish between the memories of the writer, the narrator, the reader ... and the text itself. What I call 'textual memory' (see *12*) is thus merely a working hypothesis, and is not intended to imply that the text enjoys an autonomous existence; the multiple pathways through the novel that are discovered after the first linear reading are opened up by individual acts of reading.

Claude Simon has referred to the elements of psychological realism which are still evident in *Histoire*, but which disappear in the novels of the 'third period', as an undesirable residue; 'des scories' (*3*, p.107). This, like the description of the novel as 'circular', is a retrospective comment, made after the publication of *La Bataille de Pharsale* (1969), and *Les Corps conducteurs*

(1971), in which verbal associations largely determine the sequence of textual fragments. The logic of these texts is neither linear nor circular, but based, as Stuart Sykes shows, on spatial models (see *17*, pp.126-66). *Histoire*, with its realist outer frame, is already tending towards a formal order of a spatial kind, but remains linked, via the 'memory' of the previous novels, to both the ideology and the aesthetics of literary realism. There are thus two opposed tendencies at work in the novel, the one gathering in to itself the achievements of the 'second period', and linked to autobiographical sources, and the other actively subverting the nostalgia for the past, and seeking a new aesthetic order. To read *Histoire* in the belief that it wholly respects certain conventions of psychological realism, or to interpret it in terms of 'phenomenological realism' alone, would therefore be to deny the novel an element of ambiguity essential to its deeper meanings; to read it in the way required by theoreticians of the 'new novel', such as Jean Ricardou, would be to recognise its modernity, but deny the significance of the ambiguity, by treating meanings derived from it as suspect, because originating in an ideology of art which the 'new novel' rejects. I hope to show that these alternatives are unnecessarily limiting, and that they can be mutually illuminating rather than mutually exclusive. The purpose of this chapter, for example, is to demonstrate that neither the more traditional critics, nor those associated with the 'new novel' movement, and influenced by theoretical criticism, have so far provided an adequate account of the novel.

The use of the spatial metaphor of the circle to describe *Histoire* must now be re-examined from the point of view of the reading process. Is it necessary, or helpful, for example, to imagine either the first or subsequent readings as following the same circular trajectory, A A', as Simon's diagram seems to indicate? Is there any symbolic element in this metaphor — i.e. the circle as a symbol of clock time? The only dimension of the text in which it appears to be relevant is the fictional one — the day in the life of the anonymous narrator, and in that case, the idea of circularity would appear to belong to the residue of psychological realism that the author rejects. Indeed if our reading were as 'circular' as the diagram suggests, then the conclusion would surely be that we read the *same story* in each successive reading. This certainly does not correspond to the way in which the text begins to function when we read it 'between the lines', in the way illustrated in the next chapter of this study.

It might be thought that the sequence in which the postcards appear in the text was a key to some aspect of the structure of the novel, but an examination of the dates that are provided quickly reveals this line of inquiry as unfruitful. Simon, moreover, in answer to a question on this point, at the 1974 colloquium devoted to his work, confirmed that there was no intended relationship between the order of appearance of the postcards and either the chapter sequence or the events in the narrator's day (*4*, p.17).

No one model or metaphor can therefore adequately account for *Histoire*, which must be considered as a text that will be structured only by specific acts of reading, first linear, then perhaps 'circular' — but ultimately fragmented, for once the reader begins to make connections across the text, no single order or direction can any longer be perceived: the text has broken out of both the realist 'frame', and the retrospective formal model suggested by the author. Simon's diagram, and his commentary upon the diagram are thus only useful as guides to the reader who requires the reassurance that such models provide. The diagram suggests that order and disorder exist side by side in the novel; but the novel's epigraph suggests that they alternate — as if we could not perceive them simultaneously — and that in the end, it is disorder which returns:

> Cela nous submerge. Nous l'organisons. Cela
> tombe en morceaux.
> Nous l'organisons de nouveau et tombons
> nous-mêmes en morceaux.
>
> RILKE

3. Identities

Simon described in an interview the circumstances in which he started writing *Histoire*:

> C'était un soir; j'étais assis devant ma fenêtre et j'ai commencé à décrire l'arbre que je voyais. En décrivant cet arbre j'ai parlé des oiseaux qui étaient dedans qu'on entendait confusément. J'ai revu une caricature orléaniste qui était dans mon livre d'histoire où les rois et les reines étaient figurés comme des oiseaux dans les arbres avec des couronnes de diamants. Cette image a amené d'autres images, les amies de ma grand'mère, etc. (*8*, p.189)

There was, then, it would seem, no prior plan — the novel grew out of a description, and a process of association which led Simon to the subject of his grandmother, and from there to his family in general. If, therefore, when we read *Histoire*, we assume that the narrative 'je' represents Claude Simon, we are obliged to read the whole of the novel as autobiography. Simon himself does not consider the work to be autobiographical, and we must consequently consider how to interpret the 'je', and look at the general question of identities in the novel. Without some answer to this and related questions, *Histoire* must be unreadable: if we can rely neither upon the fiction as representational (in view of the inconsistencies noted earlier), nor upon an underlying truth rooted in autobiography, we will be at a loss as to exactly *how* to read the text, let alone perceive its meanings.

The three novels that precede *Histoire* all make use of third person narration, in past tenses. *Histoire*, on the other hand, is narrated in the first person, and in spite of the ambiguity of the present participles, which can refer to both present and past, a clear temporal perspective is perceptible, as the following examples of pronominal constructions and tense usage show:

quand je travaillais; je pouvais la voir; les imaginant; pouvant entendre; dont le nom était pour moi; amenant à mon esprit; la nimbait pour moi; comme je l'avais parfois entendu faire; que je pouvais voir; j'essayai de voir; je ne pus voir que les roses; Je cherchai; lorsque je les avais touchées; où je pouvais voir; que j'avais vus; me rappelant la fois où; je vis qu'ils bougeaient; je n'eus pas le temps de lire (etc.) (pp.11-18)

Behind what may appear to be a rambling and disorganised opening to the novel we have, it would seem, a quite conventional narrative technique, employing tenses which structure the past from the point of view of the strongly marked 'je'.

When asked whether the novel was not 'une manière d'autobiographie', Simon's answer was as follows:

Je ne crois pas, non. C'est un roman. Sans doute j'utilise mes souvenirs personnels comme premiers matériaux, mais la dynamique de l'écriture et de l'imaginaire les déforme. Il y a des choses que j'ai passées sous silence, d'autres qui ont grossi. Au bout du compte, le narrateur est moi, et n'est plus moi.[4]

The 'self' whose thoughts and actions are described in *Histoire* has thus a curious dual status; like the hero-narrators of Samuel Beckett's later novels he is both 'I' and 'Not I'. Clearly, he cannot be treated as if he were a character in a conventional realist novel, since he appears to exchange identities with his uncle Charles, who in his turn becomes the narrator. If the novel represents a quest for identity, that quest must be deemed a failure: the final 'moi?', literally the last word of the text, neatly begs the whole question. If the novel purports to tell a consistent 'story' moreover, it ultimately disappoints us: the narrator withholds certain vital information which, according to the common-sense view, he would have no good reason not to provide — why, otherwise, tell the 'story' in the first place? There is

---

[4] Quoted by J. Piatier in 'Entretien: "Rendre la perception confuse, multiple et simultanée du monde"', *Le Monde* (Supplément au 6932), 26 avril 1967, p.V.

no certainty at the end of the novel, for example, as to whether anyone, other than the unknown woman mentioned in the recurrent newspaper headlines, has actually committed suicide. Who, then, is the narrator of *Histoire*? Is he an authorial 'persona', an 'implied author', or an autonomous narrator of his own 'histoire' — everyman or no-man?

The fact is that both third person and first person narration become problematic when looked at from outside the realist tradition, and from outside literature itself. The linguist Emile Benveniste, for example, described historical narrative (a definition which covers narrative fiction, where stories are narrated 'as if' they were historical fact) as emanating from a linguistically empty source, that is, the third person, defined as 'the one who is not present' when language is considered within the context of acts of communication involving a sender and a receiver of a 'message' (only a first person sender and a second person receiver can be 'present' in this sense). In a strictly pursued historical narrative there will be only third person forms:

> A vrai dire, il n'y a même plus alors de narrateur. Les événements sont posés comme ils se sont produits à mesure qu'ils apparaissent à l'horizon de l'histoire. Personne ne parle ici; les événements semblent se raconter eux-mêmes.
>
> (*1*, p.241)

Historical narrative, and third person narration in fiction, thus imply an 'absent' author, and the term 'omniscient author' employed in literary criticism can tend to draw attention away from what Benveniste perceived to be a linguistic vacuum, in which events are portrayed as just happening, with no 'voices' being heard. As a rule, when reading realist novels, we do not concern ourselves much with this 'absent' author — we know from the title page that he exists or has existed, and he may speak directly to us in the preface. Occasionally he, or a 'persona' representing him, may even intrude on the narration (Stendhal and Gide for example, both following the example of Fielding). We prefer generally, however, to forget about the ultimate source of the information we receive about the fictional world depicted, and assume that the words on the page are 'transitive' in the sense of transferring attention from them to what they signify, or refer to. Consequently, when there are ambiguities or inconsistencies at the level of reference, that is the fictional world and its inhabitants, our reading becomes less automatically 'transitive'. If, further to this, our attention is drawn to an underlying text (or one written as it were between the lines), which bears traces of a process involving associations between words, both at the level of signifiers and signifieds (more conventionally, sound and meaning), then our reading is going to be drawn into a dimension closer to the present of the writing than to the past depicted in the fiction (narrative, by definition, involves the narration of something that has already happened, except in rare cases of 'stream of consciousness' narration in the present tense). Clearly, we cannot go back to the genesis of the writing, unless we consult manuscripts and so on, but our reading can at least become more like a process of discovery than a passive consumption of the 'story'.

I shall try to illustrate this process of discovery in my next chapter, but before doing so, it is necessary to probe further into the question of the identities of the 'persons' (in both the psychological and grammatical senses) who are involved when we read a work of fiction.

For Roland Barthes, all 'persons' are 'êtres de papier':

> qui parle (dans le récit) n'est pas *qui écrit* (dans la vie) et *qui écrit* n'est pas *qui est*.[5]

What is meant here is that from the point of view of either writer or reader, whose positions are symmetrical with regard to the text, the concepts of 'author', 'narrator' and 'character' are all projections: the writer becomes an author only when he is viewed through the mediation of the text, and all the 'persons' referred to in a text depend upon each other for their illusory, or projected, existences. To examine literature as a form of linguistic communication, as Benveniste and others have done,

[5] Roland Barthes, 'Introduction à l'analyse structurale des récits', *Communications*, 8, 1966, p.20.

is therefore to highlight the way in which we attend to texts, and what is revealed by this approach, when it is directed at fiction, is the way in which realist novels (and readers who read according to realist assumptions) take the language of the text for granted, for the use of the third person conceals both the text's origin (the 'I' of the writer), and its destination (the 'you' of the reader).

With *Histoire*, it is now evident that we must make a choice, either to read the novel as a realist fiction and ignore the underlying text, as well as inconsistencies and ambiguities within the fiction (notably when the narrator and Charles seem to exchange identities), or accept the ambiguities as signs of a process of textual productivity which challenges our habits as readers, and invites us to participate in what has been called *lecture/réécriture*, or a deciphering of the text 'entre les lignes'.

If we now look at the opening pages of *Histoire*, we shall be able to see how the writing illustrates the productive processes to which we have referred.

4. *Reading* Histoire

As if to emphasise the ultimate arbitrariness of the beginning of a story, the novel begins with a paragraph with neither an initial capital nor a final full stop. Punctuation is in fact minimal in the first two pages, with only one parenthesis and a few commas to arrest the flow of words. A distinctive rhythm is nevertheless created by the repeated 'comme si' heading paragraphs two and three, and the present participles introducing paragraphs four and five, before the imperfect tense at the beginning of paragraph six ('et elles s'asseyaient'), where the images begin, as it were, to settle. Finally, in paragraph seven, the recalled scene is stabilised, and can be described at length ('assemblée non pas à vrai dire de momies' etc.).

The first sentence of the text is syntactically complete, but begins with the 'left-handed' pronominal construction 'l'une d'elles', referring back to something that must be either anterior or exterior to the text proper. We gather soon enough that the unstated referent is 'branches', and that the narrator is describing a tree, but from the outset Simon has shown that the fiction comes out of nothing, unless it is the blank page that precedes the printed text. However we interpret the opening lines of the novel, it is clear that the pronoun 'elles' points back to a void, to an *absent* referent, which is both the real tree that Simon described — inaccessible to us, the readers — and an imaginary substitute (either Simon's tree or our own, it matters little which). All that the word 'elles' stands for is therefore, at best, an absence of substance. The only substantial entity present is the word itself.

We have it on the writer's own authority that he takes great pains over the opening lines of his novels, and we should not be misled by the apparent casualness of the beginning of *Histoire*, any more than we are by the first pages of *A la recherche du temps perdu*. Indeed, like Proust's anonymous narrator, Simon's 'je' starts his narrative at night. What is visible of the tree is illuminated by *artificial* light, which makes the leaves appear 'unreal':

> ses derniers rameaux éclairés par la lampe avec leurs feuilles semblables à des plumes palpitant faiblement sur le fond de ténèbres, les folioles ovales teintées d'un vert cru irréel par la lumière électrique (p.11)

While appearing to be a descriptive passage this fictional overture in fact contains images relating directly to what Simon has referred to as 'l'acte matériel d'écrire'[6], if only the basic tools, 'plumes' and 'feuilles'. If at first we do not read these words as meaning 'pens' and 'sheets of paper' it is because we do not normally expect a *descriptive* passage to offer more than one possible reading, unless it is a symbolic one, where the symbols can be decoded according to agreed conventions or ready-made interpretations. The practice of the 'new novelists' has been to exploit increasingly the fact that most words have several possible meanings, according to the contexts in which they are used. Realism generally restricts the meanings of words to the single context appropriate to the scene being described or the action being narrated, leaving the alternative meanings in abeyance. Only in poetry do we normally expect this potential for a play of meanings to be realised, or made available to the reader. Thus one of the first lessons of *Histoire* is that the text is going to make use of multiple meanings, and that behind the literal surface of the words there are likely to be allusions and associations which, if the reader is willing to follow them, necessarily entail a partial dissolution of the 'realist illusion'.

In the preface to *Orion aveugle*, Simon illustrates how attentive he is to associations not only at the level of the sound or graphic form of words (assonances, alliterations, puns etc.) but

---

[6] See the preface to *Orion aveugle*, in which Simon describes the associative processes which guide the composition of his texts. Simon always writes with a pen and this remarkable preface reproduces his manuscript hand, as well as his own line drawing of the table at which he writes.

also at the level of meaning or references:

> Une épingle, un cortège, une ligne d'autobus, un complot, un clown, un Etat, un chapitre n'ont que (c'est à dire ont) ceci de commun: une tête. L'un après l'autre les mots éclatent comme autant de chandelles romaines, déployant leurs gerbes dans toutes les directions. Ils sont autant de carrefours où plusieurs routes s'entrecroisent. Et si, plutôt que de vouloir contenir, domestiquer chacune de ces explosions, ou traverser ces carrefours en ayant déjà décidé du chemin à suivre, on s'arrête et on examine ce qui apparaît à leur lueur ou dans les perspectives ouvertes, des ensembles insoupçonnés de résonances et d'échos se révèlent. (The pages are not numbered.)

Such then is the writer's own description of the ways in which the signifying potential of words can be realised. It is evident that the reader who wishes to explore the linguistic world opened up in this way must sacrifice certain assumptions and expectations, or else, in the case of *Histoire*, risk missing much of what it has to offer.

In looking at the opening pages of *Histoire* then, there are numerous choices to be made, but the most obvious one entails pursuing a little further the initial image of the tree. In line twelve of the first page of the text, for example, the tree seems to come to life: 'comme si l'arbre entier se réveillait'. This animation of the tree coincides with the first stirrings of the birds it contains:

> d'où parvenait de faibles froissements de faibles cris d'oiseaux endormis tressaillant s'agitant gémissant dans leur sommeil

The 'mystérieuse et délicate rumeur' in the branches is, however, not just that of the imagined birds (they are invisible to the narrator), but in the material reality of our reading it is also the sound of the words themselves, the gentle brushing sound of the repeated fricatives and sibilants ('faibles froissements', 'tressaillant s'agitant gémissant'): the text has already, in the space of a few lines, referred in a number of ways to both the writer's work on language, and the two 'faces' of language — the qualities of the words themselves, and the range of meanings they can evoke.

Paragraph two begins again with the pronoun 'elles', again anticipating its textual referent. This however has changed (the linguist Roman Jakobson has described pronouns as 'shifters' because of the instability of their referents, determined entirely by context). It now refers not to the branches of the tree but to the old ladies, friends of the narrator's grandmother, who seem still to haunt the family home.

In paragraph three, the 'invisibles frémissements' and the 'invisibles soupirs', first attributed to the birds, are now transferred to the old ladies' voices. If we consider the tree as an obvious symbol of growth we can appreciate the logic of this development. It is not just determined by 'psychological' association, that is, a plausible sequence of sense impressions, experienced by the narrator, triggering memories, as would be required in a realist interpretation. For while the whole sequence of images remains *vraisemblable* as a representation of a mental process, it shows itself to be simultaneously readable as a symbolic and metaphorical illustration of a scriptural process — the growth of a text seen as a constant ramification from the initial image of the tree.

We have seen that the noises from the tree are transformed into echoes of voices from the past, but we should perhaps consider for a moment why these voices are 'invisibles', as opposed to inaudible, which would seem to be a more appropriate description. From the point of view of the narrator both the tree and the birds are invisible outside the house — such is the plausible explanation. If, however, we look at the image of the tree as a symbol related to the writing, we can see that it represents both the growth (or 'arborescence' (see *14*, pp.124-27)) of the text, and its initial stimulus — as Simon's anecdote showed. Thus, whereas the house symbolises the narrator's mind and its contents, particularly memories of the past — that is, elements within the 'story' — the tree (which is not directly mentioned until the next section in the novel) symbolises both the autobiographical origin of the writing, and the quasi-organic creative activity of the writing.

The 'invisible' voices that the narrator of *Histoire* imagines remind us therefore of the gulf between reality and fiction, and the fact that all that is presented in a novel must pass through language. The mental pictures that are summoned up by the writing are 'distanced': the *literal* dimension of the text calls attention to itself, revealing its own peculiarly linguistic logic, and its material presence.

Whereas the conventions of realism entail the *disappearance* of language, which operates as a screen, or a window upon a represented world, the theory and the practice of writing among the 'new novelists' require that the reader reconsider the view that language is a representational medium. At the time he wrote *Histoire*, Claude Simon had not yet been wholly won over to the extreme 'materialist' view (according to which all that we 'see' in our minds while reading is illusory, the product of the idealist tendency in our culture), but the degree to which language is permitted to operate in defiance of the 'realist illusion' is characteristic of the ambiguity of *Histoire*, simultaneously a great psychological novel in the Proustian tradition, and an experimental avant-garde text.

II Voices

We can perhaps understand better now why, in paragraph three of *Histoire*, the noises from the tree are associated in the narrator's memory, with the voices of the old ladies:

> les plaintives et véhémentes protestations que persistaient à émettre les débiles fantômes bâillonnés par le temps la mort mais invincibles invaincus continuant de chuchoter ... dans ce seul registre qui leur était maintenant permis, c'est-à-dire au-dessous du silence que quelques éclats quelques faibles rires quelques sursauts d'indignation ou de frayeur crevaient parfois (p.12)

These 'voices' are 'au-dessous du silence', hushed because, as we learn shortly afterwards, the narrator's mother is dying, but also, if we now switch to our 'literal' reading, because words in a text are also 'au-dessous du silence', their aural and oral qualities present only as echoes, or remembered traces, in the reader's mind. The first characters to emerge out of the narrator's 'past' are 'débiles fantômes bâillonnés' not only because they are dead, but because like all 'persons' in fiction they are absent and speechless: their resurrection is wholly dependent upon the silent words of the text, signs that can refer only to *absent* referents, which themselves have a purely imaginary status.

The representational effect is thus only one of several possible effects that the writing can produce; the 'voices' of the old ladies, emerging out of the darkness, can be read as symbols for the past, for memory, or indeed as symbols for the infinite background murmur of language itself, always *already there*, an endless circulation of signs.

To sum up, the opening of *Histoire* incorporates an unwritten commentary upon the nature of fiction and of writing, which instead of being a transcription of speech, is revealed as the medium in which language realises itself, as a differential system, consisting of traces, or imprints, which signify only in relation to each other, having no intrinsic meaning.

So far, I have discussed issues which concern largely the problem of the genesis of the text, and metaphors connected with the activity of writing. There are, however, several more ways of looking at the first images that appear in *Histoire*. If, for example, the 'vaste maison délabrée' can be read as a metaphor for the contents of the narrator's memory (the house is of course a standard image for this and thus for the fiction as a whole), it also represents, both symbolically and realistically, that part of his past most intimately connected with it, his childhood. The house has been partly emptied of its furniture, and we learn that the narrator has only just returned there from Paris, following the (presumed) death of his wife ('Alors de nouveau parmi nous? On m'a dit...' (p.55)). The empty house is like an echo chamber:

Pouvant entendre dans le silence le pas claudiquant de la bonne traversant la maison vide (p.13)

Looked at in this way, the empty house can also stand for the
state of psychological 'absence' to which the writer regresses in
order to write, and out of which come the silent words as he
listens to the 'voices' from the past. Similarly, the reader must
suspend his attention to the world of phenomena around him, in
order to 'listen' to the text. Moreover, by stating that the old
ladies are gagged ('bâillonnées par le temps, la mort'), the text
reminds us of what we will always tend to forget — that if we imagine substantial presences (as opposed to 'débiles fantômes')
and actual voices (as opposed to traces from the past of
language), then we are submitting to an idealist illusion.
Realism, in a word, is based upon idealist assumptions; the contrary of what we are trained to believe.

III Words and Names

In his description of the circumstances in which he started
writing *Histoire*, Claude Simon referred to the way in which the
birds in the tree made him think of an illustration in the history
book he had as a child. The novel reproduces this:

> les imaginant, sombres et lugubres, perchées dans le réseau
> des branches, comme sur cette caricature orléaniste
> reproduite dans le manuel d'Histoire et qui représentait
> l'arbre généalogique de la famille royale (pp.12-13)

We have already seen that the names of the characters in
Histoire have to be treated with some caution, as a result of the
shift in priorities which has led us to treat the representation of
the fictional world in general as only one of several types of effect that the writing can produce. In an ironically Proustian
passage in paragraph five the family names of the old ladies are
contrasted with their fictional referents:

> (la vieille bonne) lançant d'une voix brusque furieuse et
> comme outragée elle aussi les noms aux consonances
> rêches médiévales — Almarik, Willum, Gouarbia — assor-
> tis de titres de générales et de marquises, puis s'effaçant
> laissant pénétrer dans leur aura d'éclatantes évocations où

chatoyaient les images de barons germaniques de
hallebardes de cités italiennes de gardénias l'un ou l'autre
de ces informes paquets de fourrures et de chiffons que
l'on voit hanter les parcs des stations thermales préoccupés
de tisanes de cataplasmes et de troubles de circulation (pp.13-14)

The narrator now comments on one of these names in particular:

cette tante de Reixach cette baronne Cerise ... dont le nom
était pour moi la source de multiples associations, affublée
d'un maquillage ridicule dont elle enluminait maladroite-
ment son visage raviné, les vieilles lèvres crevassées peintes
d'un rouge évoquant de façon bouffonne la fraîcheur du
mot cerise qu'on retrouvait aussi dans les couleurs pim-
pantes agrestes (casaque verte, manches et toque cerise) ...
le mot toque lui-même amenant à mon esprit (s'accordant
au maquillage, à la légende d'amazone, au registre aigu et
précieux de sa voix et aux coiffures emplumées qu'elle ar-
borait) le qualificatif de toquée qui paradoxalement la
nimbait pour moi d'un prestige particulier (pp.14-15)

With this passage a new and very important dimension has been
added to the text, and that is colour. I shall look at the network
of images associated with the word 'cerise' in chapter 5, but
would stress here that it is the narrator who brings it first to our
attention, and in such a way that we must conclude that the
author is now orientating our reading more explicitly than
hitherto. For the moment, the word 'cerise' remains linked to
the image of the old aunt, and to the colour red, and a general
connotation of freshness. The other example of a play on words,
'toque — toquée', entails a semantic displacement more radical
in its implications, for it shows how the character of this
'character' is derived from words. She is not an entity to whom
words are applied, but a name (a nick-name, or *made-up* name)
which produces other words.

In the remainder of paragraph six we are shown how the addition of one word to another modifies and even contradicts the first series of associations:

> son accouplement avec le mot vieille lui conférant au contraire dans mon esprit une sorte de majesté et de mystère, l'englobant dans cette aura d'obscure puissance qui les entourait toutes: vaguement fantastiques, vaguement incrédibles, retirées dans leur royale solitude, cette roide majesté qui contrastait avec leur fragilité physique, et ce privilège exclusif qu'elles détenaient, puisqu'on disait d'elles qu'elles allaient bientôt mourir, tout — jusqu'à ces maquillages maladroits — concourant á leur conférer l'aspect mythique et fabuleux d'êtres à mi-chemin entre l'humain, l'animal et le surnaturel, siégeant comme ces aéropages de créatures (juges ou divinités souterraines) qui détiennent la clef d'un monde paré du prestige de l'inaccessible (p.15)

As so often in Simon's novels, the resurrection of the past via memory is described using similes that relate to other art forms, other modes of representation; characters — like the old ladies in the passage above — are already 'personnages', as Françoise Van Rossum-Guyon noted in her contribution to the 1974 colloquium on Simon's work:

> Les personnages qui peuplent les romans de Simon apparaissent aux yeux des narrateurs, des protagonistes et, par conséquent des lecteurs, précisément comme des 'personnages': déguisés, fardés et masqués, affectant des poses théâtrales ou clownesques, jouant un role fictif et irréel.
>
> (*4*, p.98)

The effect of this aspect of Simon's technique is to draw attention to the narrative function, indeed to the act of narration itself, and in such a way that the narration can be seen not just as a vehicle for the representation of the fiction, but as an activity, through which we witness the creation of the fiction. This double focus constitutes another aspect of the underlying text that we have referred to. Like Proust, Simon frequently uses references to painting, photography and theatre, as well as cinema, in order to comment upon the artificiality of mimetic art, particularly so as to reveal how images are arrested in time. While painting and photography appear to freeze a moment in time, conferring upon it a seemingly absolute value, narrative art, whose element is time itself, cannot exist without a temporal perspective. The mental images that we produce in reading a narrative are automatically swallowed up by the past: all such images thus carry with them their own future absence; their transience is a constant reminder of mortality itself.

The 'morbidity' of much of the imagery that Simon uses, as in the description of the old ladies, is therefore not only metaphysical in character: it is related to an artistic perception — the realisation that the world of fiction (considered as a mimetic art, or according to realist criteria) is a dead one. What Simon came to realise, as he wrote *Histoire*, was that the theory and the practice of *écriture*, which allow the language of the text to accede to a productive role, could liberate both narration and fiction from the kind of theatricality that conventional representation inevitably involves.

In paragraph eight of *Histoire* there occurs what may be another oblique reference to Proust, as the narrator recalls the old ladies swallowing cakes ('molles pâtisseries'), reminiscent of the 'madeleine' that serves as the fictional pretext for the rediscovery of the past via 'la mémoire involontaire' in *Du côté de chez Swann*. The transition from paragraph eight to paragraph nine is the first example in the text of a type of switching of contexts that relies upon unstated associations, a procedure which increases throughout the novel, as the reader acquires greater familiarity with the contents of the narrator's 'memory', and his major preoccupations at the psychological level:

le furtif passage d'une langue entr'aperçue, grisâtre, grumeleuse et, aurait-on dit, adhésive comme celles de ces animaux insectivores, voraces, impassibles et précis, hap-

pant mouches et fourmis
    sorte d'organe préhensif que je pouvais voir, agenouillé
à côté de grand'mère, elle sur son prie-Dieu (p.16)

The image of the tongue, as I shall show later, introduces a
dimension of *Histoire* which could be satisfactorily explored
only in a psychoanalytical study. For the present, it serves as a
means by which the text arrives at the subject that dominates the
first part of the novel, if not the novel as a whole: the figure of
the narrator's mother, on her death-bed, taking communion.
The religious context in the fiction conceals, however, another
level of commentary, again concerned with language — as if, in
fact, the word *langue* had called up, among other things, the
idea of 'language' as well as 'tongue' in the sense of the speech
organ itself — for the description of the death-bed scene con-
tinues with the narrator's account of his attempt to *read* the
Greek letters (spelling out of name of Christ) on the priest's
robe. As we shall see in chapter 6 the fascination with words in
foreign tongues is closely linked with erotic themes in the novel,
and thus also with the female characters, including the mother.
In fact, what we come across in paragraphs eight and nine is in
many ways the imaginative nexus of the novel, involving images
relating to the mother, to death, to sex and to language. Why
language should be a central issue in a scene depicting the narrator's childhood memories of his dying mother is thus now
becoming apparent: the practice of *écriture*, by making the
represented fictional world into just one of the potential effects
produced by the text, allows a return to desires latent in us all,
and deepest among them the repressed instincts which, in the unconscious, still attach us to our first erotic object. The loosening
of the relationship between words and their more obvious meanings allows the text to function rather like a dream, and, like
dreams, to achieve the symbolic realisation of hidden desires. A
text like *Histoire* cannot be contained within traditional defini-
tions of narrative fiction, for in it language has broken out of
the mould imposed by realism, and is beginning to function in
an authentically poetic way.
    The transition from paragraph eight to paragraph nine again

relies upon the word *langue*, but this time applied to the pistils of
the flowers that bedeck the mother's room:

> amoncelées, exubérantes, dardant leur espèce de langue
> jaune érectile comme de la peluche, pollen couleur de
> safran qui m'était resté sur les doigts lorsque je les avais
> touchées (p.17)

The death-bed scene can thus be seen to refer indirectly to the
child's initiation into language, and the concomitant renuncia-
tion of the exclusive love of the mother that is the price that the
child pays when it enters into the symbolic relationships that are
articulated in language. The scene clearly concentrates upon the
Word, and the Book (at the expense of the mother): 'les pages
décorées de majuscules dorées parmi les roses peintes' (p.17).
Beneath the surface of the painful description of loss at the emotional level is the story of the writer's rediscovery of his medium,
but the release of the signifying potential of language that is
repressed in realist writing involves breaking not only representational conventions, but also the theological guarantee upon
which our culture rests: the Word as Law is desacralised and
deformed, as Lambert's obscene variants on the catechism later
show (e.g. pp.48-49). As Joyce demonstrated in *Portrait of the
Artist as a Young Man* and *Ulysses*, to write authentically about
the past, and cultural, historical and family pressures, involves
revolt and exile. *Histoire* is, however, ambiguous on this issue,
for the more obvious 'révolté' is Lambert, the brash, sneering
and disrespectful school companion, and later, it appears,
orthodox marxist, trotting out the revolutionary clichés, but not
getting involved, as the narrator did, in revolutionary violence.
The narrator presents himself as naive and inexperienced in contrast to Lambert, but more aware of historical forces and con-
tradictions, because his bourgeois background — the big house
and its relics of a gracious past — has meant that in order to
revolt, and run off to Barcelona, he has had to betray his class.
The fragmentary scenes in which the narrator's cousin Corinne
and her husband de Reixach allude scathingly to his misplaced
idealism illustrate clearly the historical trap that he is in, as do

his uncle Charles's sympathetic, but ironic questions and comments.

Histoire bears witness to the major revolutions of the twentieth century (e.g. the quotations from John Reed's account of the October Revolution, *Ten Days that Shook the World*), but places them in a context of cyclical global upheavals, reminding us of the epigraph of *Le Palace*:

> Révolution: Mouvement d'un mobile qui, parcourant une courbe fermée, repasse successivement par les mêmes points.

The past is not denied in *Histoire*, but while the fictional narrator remains enclosed within the world of his family past, represented by the house, the writer is engaged in transforming its content into the source of a fiction. The dynamic properties of the writing, which I have illustrated in this chapter, are weaning the text away from the past (in the sense of a ready-made story waiting to be told, a mere repetition of what has gone before), and producing new and unexpected effects. Neither the writer's personal past, nor the fictional narrator's memories are negated in the process, for both become part of a texture of resonances characterised by an artistic energy which contradicts the ostensible pessimism of the novel, described by Eduardo Sanguinetti as 'un chef d'œuvre funèbre'.

5. The Family

I Authorship and paternity

No single feature of *Histoire* can be studied in total isolation from others, for to pick out 'themes' is to beg the question of the relationship between narrative form and fictional content. We have already seen how fictional objects — the house and the tree — are transformed by the text into metaphors relating to the production of both narration and fiction: voices emanate from them, and the narrator listens. The novel grows out of linguistic elements generated by 'l'acte matériel d'écrire'. This process will be greatly reinforced by the first descriptions of the postcards, themselves the original stimulus for the writing (the description of the tree was more of a pretext, a way of getting started on the novel proper):

> L'œuvre est partie d'une collection de cartes postales adressées à ma mère et que j'ai retrouvées dans une commode. Elles m'ont fait — comment dire? — 'saliver'. En essayant de les décrire, j'ai composé une vingtaine de pages … Puis ces vingt pages, peu à peu, ont gonflé.[7]

Given what I have said about the autobiographical element in *Histoire*, we have to consider now the nature of the 'pacte' (or reading conventions) which determines our attitude towards the 'Family' presented in the novel. Do we read it with the feeling that we are going to discover something about the writer's personal life, or do we read it as fiction? Is it even a question of such neat alternatives?

Before attempting to answer these questions, we should look very briefly at patterns of family relationships in some of Simon's earlier novels, for it is apparent that right from *Le*

[7] In interview with Piatier (see note 4, p.30).

Tricheur (1946), the author's attitude towards his characters (his 'authority' over them) allows us to speak in terms of a problem of 'paternity' in both the fictional situations and the relationship between the writer and his imaginary progeny.

Louis, the delinquent anti-hero of *Le Tricheur*, is a war orphan, desperate to free himself from the stranglehold exerted upon him by his past. He attempts to run away from his memories, both literally and figuratively, and to escape from the emotional tangles of families, moral responsibilities, and bourgeois conformity. All the paths that he follows are however ultimately circular, and his last futile gesture, the gratuitous murder of a priest (a symbolic father), brings him back face to face with his oedipal fixations. Traces of oedipal patterns run through Simon's novels up until as recently as *Triptyque* (1973) (see *12*), and it is evident that Simon's increasing scepticism, over the years, regarding the conventions of fiction (such as separate identities of characters), caused him, from quite early on, to refer, ironically and indirectly, to the question of the writer's 'authority' over his characters. In *Le Sacre du printemps*, for example, the demotion of the 'implied author', or narrator within the fiction representing the writer, is beginning to become apparent, for two narrators eventually compete in telling the story. Bernard Mallet (a phonetic anagram of Hamlet) is intensely jealous of his step-father, the 'usurper' who has taken his dead father's place in his mother's bed. The rivalry between them involves then sexual jealousy, but also the boy's gradual realisation that his step-father's experience does give him the right to give advice, and try to help him sort out his adolescent problems. It is thus the step-father who wins the contest, but not before he has ironically demolished the whole basis upon which his right to take over the narration of the story was founded: as an authorial 'persona', he is pointing towards the ultimate collapse of the conventions governing the respective roles of the writer and his characters (including narrators within the fiction) which occurs in the novel which followed *Histoire*, *La Bataille de Pharsale* (1969).

This gradual evolution, in Simon's novels, towards narratorless texts (*Triptyque*, and *Leçon de choses*) corresponds closely to what Roland Barthes described as the 'death of the author' in the modern novel,[8] but the theme of the absent father also coincides with biographical fact. Like Camus, and Roland Barthes, Claude Simon belongs to a fatherless generation: their history originates in the slaughter of the 1914-1918 war. Simon's work is resonant with that primordial loss. *Le Sacre du printemps*, for example, describes graphically the effect of such a loss upon the *memory* of the principal character:

> la mémoire doutant d'elle-même ramène, moi et pas moi en même temps, des fragments de vitres cassées à travers lesquelles je peux prendre conscience ou plutôt ranimer un monde à l'échelle de l'enfant que je sais moi dans la mélancolique lumière, le mélancolique, poussiéreux, amer parfum des choses qui furent, puis cette absence, la présence de cette absence au fur et à mesure de laquelle s'effaçait le souvenir remplacé par quelque chose d'inquiétant, mystérieux, mythique, sans consistance réelle et qui tout à coup, au visage souvenir des photographies, aux images embuées de la mémoire, opposa la précise, la nouvelle réalité (*Le Sacre du printemps*, pp.31-32)

It can be seen from such an example that the central place that is occupied by memory in Simon's novels during the first and second 'periods' is directly related to a paradox — 'la présence de cette absence' — that is, to a void that can only be temporarily filled, and then by increasingly mythical images. The memory, the only guarantee of identity ('l'enfant que je sais moi'), is constantly threatened; the father, already no more than an image, a photograph (the 'visage souvenir'), is being effaced by the new reality. At a psychological level, the need to defend the father's image is thus closely linked to the need to retain a sense of identity. At an artistic level the writer's preoccupation with memory then becomes the source of an increasingly acute conflict between technical problems (such as using a narrator's memory as the only apparent source of fictional material), and a probably unconscious need to remain in contact with the lost progenitor.

[8] Roland Barthes, 'La mort de l'auteur', *Mantéia*, V, fin 1968.

The writer's formal choices, it would seem, are dictated by psychological factors: Claude Simon's experiments with narrative, and his aesthetic quest remain rooted — at least up until *Histoire* — in his personal history.

Simon, as we have seen, admits a degree of ambivalence in the novel ('le narrateur est moi et n'est plus moi'), and he approaches the issue of whether or not the characters presented are members of his own family by appealing to the generalising power of art:

> tout le monde a une cousine, tout le monde mange des cerises, etc. L'autobiographie, il me semble, réclame plus de singularité. Mais peut-être, comme disait Gide, est-ce en approfondissant le particulier qu'on atteint l'universel. Or moi je tends à l'universel.[9]

If it were indeed true that were we dealing with an autobiographical family in *Histoire*, we would expect, according to the conventions of autobiography, to be able to name the members of the author's family, and see them united under the patronym. Instead, the narrator remains anonymous: neither forename nor surname is supplied; the move from the particular to the universal thus involves the *suppression* of certain names, as well as the substitution of fictional names for real ones.

In a passage near the beginning of the novel that we have already looked at, the name 'de Reixach' occurs (p.14). The first act of recognition by the reader of *Histoire* acquainted with Simon's previous novels will therefore cause him to think of another text: *La Route des Flandres*; an 'intertextual' element thus enters immediately into the general question of identities, and we can thus perceive, if we can resist sufficiently the blandishments of our 'realist' tendencies, that the referent of this name is not so much a person (or 'character'), as a word — but a particular type of word, for names, as Proust so brilliantly showed, in 'Noms de pays: le nom', have a particular appeal to the imagination:

---

[9] In interview with Piatier (see note 4, p.30).

Mais les noms présentent des personnes — et des villes
qu'ils nous habituent à croire individuelles, uniques comme des personnes — une image confuse, qui tire d'eux, de
leur sonorité éclatante ou sombre, la couleur dont elle est
peinte uniformément (*Du côté de chez Swann,* Coll. Folio,
pp.458-59)

The name 'de Reixach' (pronounced 'ryshack') is followed by
a reference to one of his aunts, nick-named 'Baronne Cerise'.
We saw earlier how the 'multiples associations' produced by this
name were attributed to the narrator as a child (much in the
same way that Proust goes on to describe the effects produced in
his narrator, 'Marcel', as a boy, by the place-names 'Parme' and
'Florence', and thence to link the desire to visit these places with
sentimental and erotic desire in general). We saw also how these
recalled associations related to the writing, and to the source of
its productivity: the generation of associations at the level of
both the signifier (aspect and sound) and the signified (reference
or meaning). Already, in *La Route des Flandres*, the word
'cerise' was linked to the name 'de Reixach', for Corinne, his
glamorous widow, is frequently described as wearing cherry-
coloured dresses (for examples, *La Route des Flandres*, p.147).
In that novel, the word 'cerise' operates as a trigger for erotic
associations, and these associations are clearly carried over into
Histoire. However, at the beginning of *Histoire* the word 'cerise'
is singled out some time *before* the character of Corinne appears
— and then she is presented as a small girl (there is no mention,
in *Histoire*, of the erotic encounter between 'Georges' and
Corinne in *La Route des Flandres*). The way in which *Histoire*
treates names thus indicates already how the writing has taken
precedence over the fiction. Freed from explicit autobiographical references, with the narrator relegated to a position
where he is now no more than a support for the fictional pretext
(that of telling a 'story'), the writing can exploit more openly the
linguistic material which is in the process of taking over the production of both the narration and the fiction.

II The Mother

The associations produced by the word 'cerise' include, as we
saw earlier, the colour 'red'. In the description of the dying
mother's room, there are several references to roses — bunches
of roses in the room, roses embroidered on the priest's robe, and
rose garlands in the motif on the carpet. There are also drops of
blood embroidered on the priest's robe, at the point where the
flowers create a crown around the sacred heart. The specific colour of the roses is not mentioned, but if we look just at the word
in the text, 'rose', we can see that it can signify (among other
things), a shade of red. The drops of blood being symbols of
death, the sacrifice of the son for the father (also the maternal
love included in the many meanings associated with the image of
the sacred heart), we can begin to appreciate how powerful a
force of attraction and suggestion can be generated by the colour
red. The links between these images are, however, not specific:
they are produced in the writing by an overflow of connotations
from one image to another.

If we now look at the way in which the figure of the mother is
presented, we see that the associations we have mentioned con-
tribute to the creation of a powerful complex of meanings —
again, non-specified, operating at a level of deferred connections, which are made only by acts of reading which keep open
the multiple pathways of what the theorists of *écriture* have
called *signifiance*, or open, sliding meanings.

The image of the mother is treated throughout much of the
novel with an almost fearful deference. At first she is only
glimpsed, and what strikes the narrator (as a child) is the emacia-
tion of her features:

> son visage comme une lame de couteau vue de face le nez
> aussi comme une lame de couteau avec en haut de chaque
> côté les deux yeux noirs brillants puis tout revint en place et
> son visage disparut lui aussi tandis qu'il se dirigeait de
> nouveau vers le livre les onduleuses stries couleur de lilas
> fané passant de gauche à droite puis je les eus de nouveau
> juste en face de moi gouttes de Son Sang disait-il (p.19)

The boy's gaze follows the strings of embroidered roses on the back of the priest's vestment, up until they meet at 'le carrefour la couronne le coeur'. This alliterative cluster displays the activity of the writing at the level of both form and meaning, for it designates explicitly the coming together of multiple associations at both levels, and the way in which words can operate as 'crossroads', or meeting places for the pathways opened up by the relaxation of the controls upon which realism depends. The priest's tonsured head then suddenly disappears from view, as he bends towards the mother, and the boy imagines him as a decapitated martyr. At this moment, above the priest's shoulder, he sees the portrait on the wall which will slightly later be identified as that of his dead father:

> souriant comme une de ces apparitions entourées d'un halo de lumière ... semblable à quelque divinité au système pileux soyeux et bouclé (p.20)

The whole description is eminently 'phenomenological', following carefully, in a realistic sequence, the movements of the priest, and recording the restricted field of vision of the boy, while also narrating his fantasies. There is, however, much more: in the images describing the mother, the priest and the father, there is an associative chain which links the knife blade ('son visage comme une lame de couteau') to blood, tonsuring and decapitation, and to the depiction of the father as 'semblable à quelque divinité au système pileux soyeux et bouclé', in contrast to the tonsured priest. The tonsuring of the priest being the symbolic equivalent of castration, and the martyrdom of saintly figures being re-enactments of Christ's self-sacrifice (the Son for the Father), it is evident that the appearance of the father's head (likened to that of a god), on the priest's shoulders, can be related to oedipal fantasies. The fact that the image of the knife appears in the description of the mother adds a further layer to the significance of the scene, for with the father's death the mother has become the figure wielding the symbolic power to castrate, and punish incestuous impulses: she is what is known in psychoanalytical theory as the 'phallic mother', and this explains the fear she seems to arouse in the boy — quite apart from the fact that, because of her illness, she is a frightening figure.

III The Father

The father in *Histoire* is not even a memory: he is nothing more than a name and an image; the 'énorme agrandissement' of a photograph, hanging on the wall, emphasises his purely mythical status.

The ambivalence of the boy's unconscious feelings are, moreover, reflections of the very transformations of *real* feelings that occur in the process of writing; the absence of the parents, for the narrator, alone in 'la vaste maison délabrée', is echoed by the absence of the fictional referents, forever sliding away beneath the material presence of the words themselves. Perhaps this is why the boy tries to *read* the Greek letters on the priest's vestments (spelling out the word 'Christos') and the Latin inscription INRI (Iesus Nazarenus Rex Iudaeorum), itself so close, phonetically, to the father's christian name, Henri, which is given a little later.[10] *Histoire*, seen in this way, does indeed tell a 'universal' story — that of the mourning process that the death of parents involves for every human being.

It is significant also that the chain of memories that leads back to the evocation of the narrator's parents breaks off at this point, and the text switches to descriptions of the postcards sent by the father to the mother during his travels. Death, it seems, presents a barrier which neither psychological nor phenomenological realism can bridge: the novel has only one option — to describe fragmentary memories, images and mementos, to *imagine* (make into images) the parents to whom the text is addressed. There is no route back into the past, only the future of the text to come.

[10] See *Nouveaux problèmes du roman*, Editions du Seuil, 1978, pp.262-65; where Jean Ricardou has used the example of these initials to demonstrate how a text can illustrate aspects of its own transformational and productive processes. He sees INRI as an anagrammatical variant on 'rien', and thus as an emblem of the creation of the text *ex nihilo*, and its subsequent elaboration on the basis of its own material elements. The 'rien' that Ricardou's reading produces is, I would suggest, equally applicable to the void of the authorless text and the theme of the fatherless son.

Histoire, once again, attains to the 'universal' by narrating what can only ever be a mythical account of origins and endings, but it transcends the 'roman familial' which psychoanalytical criticism sees as the basis of so many novels (representing fantasies expressing the desire to have been born of *other* parents), by remaining true to a core of personal memories — it is both particular *and* universal, and, as such, achieves a stature that can be matched by few modern texts.

The narrator's discovery of the postcards thus achieves several things simultaneously: they provide a visual and a linguistic stimulus for the narration of his imaginary version of the long drawn-out period following his parents' betrothal and eventual marriage, while also serving to paper over the gaps in the narrator's story — what he cannot know about his parents, but what, unconsciously, he wants most of all to know: the circumstances of his conception. Here again, we reach a level of universal fantasy, given a quality of particular intensity as a result of the father's death: to be the child of an imaginary father is to be, in a sense, an imaginary child, and to be a prey to fantasies of de-realisation. The narrator's inner emptiness thus relates back, beyond the loss of his mother, and then his wife, to the need to find the father he has never known. The satisfaction of that need is, however, never likely to be achieved, since all that he can hope to find is a grave on a battle-field.

A description of what we conclude to be the father's tomb occurs on page 384, and it is again significant that the gap between writing and reality is accentuated by firstly the anonymity of the grave, and secondly, the fact that it is 'visited' via a photograph, a postcard representation, which is, moreover, slightly blurred (we will see in chapter 7 the importance of the blurred photograph of Van Velden's studio). The passage occurs as one of a series of short paragraph blocks relating to the seemingly parallel circumstances surrounding the death of Charles's wife, and the narrator's wife Hélène, and describes a fresh grave, a mound of earth on which grass and weeds are beginning to grow. After a brief erotic sequence, which, because of certain recurrent images, we associate with Hélène, the narrator reflects upon what has taken her place — nothing but 'un nom gravé sur

une dalle'. This is a transition point for the writing, and the next
sequence takes up the motif of the name, but in a negative way:

> et pour lui même pas de nom tombe anonyme cette carte
> que quelqu'un avait envoyée LUZY (Meuse) Cimetière
> hémicirculaire élevé par les Allemands pendant l'occupa-
> tion ... Derrière la grille de fer on pouvait voir un chêne
> poussant au milieu des tombes sans doute faisait-il un léger
> vent une partie de son feuillage bougeait chaque feuille
> faisant sur la photographe une courte traînée oblique floue
> toutes dans le même sens comme des hachures on pouvait
> entendre chanter des oiseaux (pp.416-17)

The paragraph which follows describes what the narrator imagines to have been his mother's reaction:

> trop épuisée sans doute ou peut-être sa tête le cimetière
> parmi d'autres vues banales envoyées par des amis en
> voyages indifférentes ou peut-être indifférente elle-même
> avant ou après quelle importance puisque tout était arrêté
> maintenant présent immobilisé tout là dans un même mo-
> ment à jamais les images les instants les voix les fragments
> du temps du monde multiple fastueux inépuisable épar-
> pillés sur un lit de mourante (p.417)

At this moment, time and history itself stopped for the
mother, and thus, in a sense, for her son also. If fiction can no
longer build upon historical models, and is searching for a new
order, it is because the only guarantor of the old order — the
Family, representing security, the transmission of values, in-
stituted meanings — has ceased to have any secure foundation.
All that remains is the old house, and a bundle of postcards —
representing a world that has fragmented into myriad images.

The card announcing the father's death (in writing this time)
surfaces a few pages later:

> J'apprends qu'Henri a été tué Que vous dire Vous écrirai
> dès que cela me sera possible Nous traversons en ce

moment un des passages les plus critiques de la guerre mais
le bon droit vaincra Nous le vengerons Mes respectueux
sentiments ainsi qu'à Madame votre mère Colonel Le
Magnien Secteur 212

puant sans doute les orbites vides des lambeaux de chair
de cuir racorni adhérant encore par endroits les crânes des
bœufs Betsiléos surmontant un tumulus herbeux posés sur
une claie de branchages ... (p.419)

The reality of the event is again concealed, behind words this
time, patriotic slogans which emphasise the tragic waste of life
that the 'Great War' involved. The grave that the narrator imagines, moreover, is not his father's — imagination takes over,
in order to approach obliquely what the writing can never touch.

In the new order, that of the text, the past of 'History' exists
only as fragments and traces. As the American critic David
Carroll remarks, 'it is only through a complex process of construction, and reconstruction, that the novel takes form in terms
of this material — an open, non-fictionalised form, constantly
calling attention to its own limitations and instability' (2, p.807).
The postcards, and the memories of the photographic portrait,
are all that remain.

IV Substitutes

The Family in *Histoire* includes of course a father-substitute,
and (though of lesser importance) a mother-substitute: uncle
'Charles' and 'grand'mère'. I shall consider later the curious
substitutions that occur between the narrator and Charles, but
first of all it is worth pointing out that 'Charles' is a somewhat
ambiguous figure from very early on in the novel, as the conversation between the narrator and the old man he meets on the
street before going into the bank (in Section III) reveals:

Ce pauvre Charles: avec les femmes il était d'une naïveté!
..., puis de nouveau s'immobilisant, attendant, tandis que
ses yeux continuaient à m'examiner, sournois, rusés, puis
la voix se faisant de nouveau entendre: Cette fille, elle le

> trompait avec tout le monde, c'était ...
>> et moi: Quelle fille?
>> et lui: Comment: quelle ... Vous ne ... Mais je croy-
>> ais que ...
>> et moi: Mais bien sûr. Voyons, je sais (pp.76-77)

In this allusive discussion of Charles's affair with an artist's model there is some initial confusion about the identity of the girl in question, and if we are reading in a 'realist' way, we will assume that the question 'Quelle fille?' refers only to Charles's mistress. However, in the passage that follows, in answer to a question (elided in the text) put to him by the old man, the narrator says 'Oui ravissante'. There is no way of knowing, initially, to whom he is referring, but it rapidly emerges that the old man has asked for news of the narrator's cousin Corinne:

> sa vieille voix gluante me rappelant maintenant comme Corinne était jolie qu'il n'avait jamais vu une jeune fille aussi c'était comment dire, et moi essayant de me dégager ... disant Oui c'est une tradition de famille chez nous Je veux dire le veuvage Une de ces maladies de femme vous savez Congénitale comme on dit Oui Transmissible aux hommes du clan par voie utérine, lui me regardant méfiant perplexe se demandant s'il devait rire ou quoi (p.77)

The narrator, in these exchanges, pretends for a moment not to know about Charles's affair, but this question, 'Quelle fille?' reveals already the identification with his uncle which leads to the ambiguities of the latter part of the novel. It can be seen, moreover, in this example, that it is also the *writing* that is asking the question: this ironic confusion of identities is part of the process by which the text is freeing itself from realist representation. The immediate consequence, in the scene quoted, is a *glissement* from the ostensible subject of the conversation — Charles's mistress — to the unstated, and apparently *censured* parallels in the narrator's own life — a similar affair, perhaps, but behind it also a continuing erotic obsession with his cousin Corinne (looked at from the point of view of the fiction, the encounter between 'Georges' and Corinne in *La Route des Flandres* has also been 'censured'). Once again, a plausible 'psychological' explanation is doubled by an effect arising out of the writing process itself. The way in which this process, if uncontrolled, could lead ultimately to a complete breakdown in fictional identities is ironically underlined in the narrator's comments about widowhood ('Une de ces maladies de femme vous savez Congénitale comme on dit Oui transmissible aux hommes du clan par voie utérine'). In an article already referred to, I have shown how this risk is present in Simon's novels as early as *Le Tricheur* (*12*, p.159).

The image of the mother reappears shortly after the conversation with the old man outside the bank, in the narrator's immediate and more distant memories, jumbled together in the present of remembrance:

> Votre délicieuse mère réduite à l'état de lame de couteau
> fardée de rouge géranium (p.86)

The narrator remembers someone having said that her appearance was frightening:

> j'entendis quelqu'un dire qu'elle était à faire peur pensant
> faire-part pensant qu'on enverrait ces cartons bordés de
> noir où ont la douleur de vous fait part de la mort de leur
> mère fille soeur tante cousine pieusement décédée en sa
> quarante-cinquième peut-être sixième au maximum année
> (p.86)

The play on 'fair peur' which produces 'faire part' leads into an anticipation of the mother's death — another indication of the way the writing now determines both narration and fiction — but the borderline between life and death, given the mother's physical deterioration, is hard to determine:

> le problème étant combien de temps un organisme vivant
> peut-il continuer à fonctionner lorsqu'il reste sur les os un
> simple sac de peau enfermant non plus les organes

habituels foie estomac poumons et caetera mais rien
d'autre que de la pâte à papier sous forme de vieilles cartes
postales et de vieilles lettres nouées en paquets par des
faveurs aux teintes suaves fanées, rien qu'un vieux sac
postal bosselé (p.86)

This sequence brings us to the first appearance of the question
which will recur, in an increasingly anguished way, throughout
the novel, but particularly towards the end, and which constitutes one of the most striking motifs of *Histoire*: 'Mais ex-
actement?' It is a question which not only states and repeats the
manifest impossibility of ever remembering precisely and in
detail the scenes from the past which rise into consciousness and
sink back into oblivion again as the mind is assailed by other
phenomena, past and present, but which also states, and
restates, the artistic message of the text: writing, words on
paper, can never reproduce the living presence of the dead. Just
as the mother is reduced to a packet of old postcards, so human
time, and lived experience are, in novels, 'rien d'autre que de la
pâte à papier'.

The image of the knife is thus a symbol of death and the pain
of separation, as well as being associated with oedipal fantasies,
as another remarkable passage, shortly afterwards, clearly
shows:

veuf mot boiteux tronqué restant pour ainsi dire en suspens
coupé contre nature comme l'anglais half moitié sectionné
cut of [*sic*] coupé de quelque chose qui manque soudain
dans la bouche les lèvres prononçant VF continuant à faire
fff comme un bruit d'air froissé déchiré par le passage
rapide étincelant et meurtrier d'une lame (pp.91-92)

Although this paragraph block occurs in the context of
memories of Charles, it applies equally to the narrator himself.
The knife blade, moreover, is now what cuts off the language
(written) from its referents — both sounds (speech) and what
they represent: it symbolises the gap between fiction and reality
which realist literature tries unsuccessfully to close and the tragic

view of life which is entailed in the deterministic and fatalistic outlook that conventional narrative form imposes upon the moment-to-moment flux of existence. By the same token, the knife can, at a stroke, free the writing from realist constraints — but at what price? It would seem that however tempting the theory and practice of *écriture* may appear at the intellectual and aesthetic levels, such a 'liberation' must be measured against what is lost: a resonance, a power of suggestion, and an emotional intensity which have been matched by few modern novels.

V The Family as an Institution

Histoire treats the Family as a moribund institution, hanging desperately on to the vestiges of bourgeois respectability and an anachronistic view of the world and the historical process. If the narrator's quest ends in failure, it is because it takes place within a structure which can no longer enclose and protect a sense of identity. This structure is dependent upon the preservation of memories, in the face of all the evidence provided by History (war, death, destruction, the reversal of Order), by means of photographs, portraits, and documents which seek to underwrite the uniqueness of that identity. As David Carroll remarks, in his very helpful article on *Histoire*:

> the family home thus becomes the space of memory, the frame which encloses the novel is the guarantee of the originality and the autonomy of the subject inscribed there. (*2*, p.808)

Carroll is right to see that house as a powerful symbol for the defunct unity of the family, and to observe that its history is 'more about conflict, absence, and discontinuity than about harmony, presence and continuity' (*2*, pp.808-9).

The family presented in *Histoire* is clearly under the sign of death: there is an almost symmetrical reduction occurring through the four generations represented: a grandmother (but no grandfather), a dying mother (and a dead father), two widowers (Charles and the narrator), and a widow (Corinne).

The situations of Charles and the narrator are thus strictly
parallel, and those of the narrator and Corinne illustrate what
one could call a negative complementarity. The only intact family unit remaining is that of the narrator's cousin Paulou. That
his little daughter should be called Corinne (the appearance of
the name on page 326 causes a brief moment of confusion, or
'delayed revelation') seems to be yet another proof of the way in
which the text reverts, beneath the realist surface, to the censured objects of its desire — a bundle of erotic motifs (cherries,
red colours, chocolate, etc.) which congregate around the name
'Corinne' — which literally encloses the notion of a *body* (corps-
Corinne), or to push the play on words suggested by the text a
little further, a *corpus* of circulating words and meanings. These
erotic motifs are not allowed to surface explicitly in the text, for
as we noted earlier there are no erotic scenes involving the
character Corinne (as in *La Route des Flandres*), since the ostensible focus of the narrator's erotic memories is his wife Hélène.
We shall see subsequently, however, that even when sexual
memories are explicitly linked to 'Hélène', the text betrays the
narrator, and 'Corinne' appears 'entre les lignes'.

VI *The Mother again*

Like the text of *Histoire* itself, we must now return to the
figure of the mother, for logically enough, with the failure of the
quest for the father, the novel comes to an end by going back to
the beginning — to the embryonic narrator, and the point where
the myth of identity upon which the fiction and the narration depend is left as a question mark over the whole enterprise (in this
respect the novel is indeed 'circular'):

> regardant écrire sur un coin de table ou de comptoir la
> femme penchant son mystérieux buste de chair blanche
> enveloppé de dentelles ce sein qui déjà peut-être me portait
> dans son ténébreux tabernacle sorte de têtard gélatineux
> lové sur lui-même avec ses deux énormes yeux sa tête de ver
> à soie sa bouche sans dents son front cartilagineux
> d'insecte, moi? ... (pp.434-5)

Although the mother is presented as a frightening figure 'cadavérique et fardée ... Polichinelle à l'aspect terrifiant et risible' (pp.67-68), associated by the recurrent image of the knife to oedipal fears, there are a number of passages which express less ambivalent feelings and, given the funereal context, add great emotional depth to the novel, the more so since they appear in fragments, and in unexpected and indirect ways. For example, at the end of section VII of the novel, after a scene in which the young narrator is humiliated before his uncle by Lambert, their exchanges come to an abrupt end as he explains why they must not raise their voices: 'ma maman est malade dis-je' (p.242). There is no further comment, and in an immediate transition to a description of the house in the darkening shadows, all the latent emotion in that brief remark is transposed, without explicit connections, into the noise of a banging shutter:

Les ténèbres envahissant la vieille maison commençant par le bas s'élevant comme une marée noire glaciale le vent hurlait par moments sous les portes il y avait toujours quelque part un volet mal fixé qui grinçait sur ses charnières cognait contre le mur et se rabattait grinçait de nouveau après un moment de silence le son était différent selon qu'il s'écartait du mur ou s'en approchait quelquefois les deux grincements semblaient lutter alternant parfois il se passait un moment pendant lequel on n'entendait rien puis il semblait pousser un gémissement aigu bref et frappait violemment le mur (p.242)

6. A Tragic Love Story

The 'story' that *Histoire* tells (or fails to tell) is one of pain and guilt and the consuming desire to re-live moments of physical ecstasy that have gone, and cannot be re-created, for the illusion that realist fiction sustains, that of re-living experience vicariously, is definitively shattered by the writing. In this chapter I shall show how in some of the most explicitly erotic passages in the novel, the text designates its own activity, and proposes linguistic material as a focus for the desire that underlies creativity, in place of the symbolic objects of realist fiction.

Love is treated very obliquely in *Histoire*: whatever caused the narrator and Hélène's separation, and perhaps her death, has already happened. The memories of the marriage are fragmentary and highly elliptical. The same is true of what we take to have been uncle Charles's parallel situation. All that we learn concerning Charles is second-hand, the information upon which the narrator's reconstruction is based being gossip, letters, postcards and the photograph of Van Velden's studio which will be the subject of my last chapter.

The separation of the narrator and Hélène is first alluded to in a fragment near the beginning of the novel (pp.44-45), where the couple face each other on a station platform. The image 'lac de larmes' describing Hélène's eyes, which comes back, again and again, at the end of the novel, derives from the first image in the text, the tree, which, as we saw, produced first the birds and then the old ladies' voices. Seeking to express his pain, the narrator tries to remember the name of the lake associated with the ferocious birds which attacked Hercules during on of his labours ('Stymphale'). The unstated reference is to the story of Hercules's encounter with the centaur Nessus, who gave Deianeira, Hercules's wife, a poisoned love potion, with which she covered his tunic. The poison rotted his flesh, and on tearing off the tunic, he tore away his own flesh. The names of Hercules and Deianeira occur only once each in the novel, the former in an ironic description of a strip cartoon in the newspaper the narrator reads in the café (p.359), and the latter in one of the last restatements of the narrator's desire to tear away the memory of his separation from Hélène, and (presumably) the guilty memories which he has suppressed:

> je voudrais, je voudrais je voudrais si je pouvais l'enlever l'arracher de moi retrouver la fraîcheur l'oubli Déjanire
> les coins de sa bouche tremblant légèrement s'abaissant se relevant de façon imperceptible très vite me regardant les yeux arrondis noirs brillants je dis Mais nous ne pouvons pas nous perdre (pp.395-6)

There is an indirect allusion to the narrator's guilt feelings during the early scene in which he washes, and ironically repeats fragments of religious liturgy (a typically Joycean device):

> la regardant s'échapper entre les doigts mal joints et à la fin plus rien que quelques minuscules gouttelettes accrochées à la peau comme sur les plumes rosâtres d'un canard. Coupe enchantée se vidant au fur et à mesure qu'on l'emplit. Ou plutôt cupule. Culpa mia. Pardonnez-moi mon indignité ainsi soit... (p.50)

The paronomastic play which produces 'culpa' from 'coupe' passes through 'cupule', a botanical term designating the sheath which holds, for example, an acorn, and 'gland' is one of the many popular synonyms for penis in French. 'Cupule' being very close to 'copule', it is evident that the word-play is of a sexual kind, and that the narrator's guilt probably relates to some extra-marital affair, which may have caused the break-down of his marriage.

Clearly, *Histoire* does not deal with 'romantic' love, but with physical desire: sensual longing, and not sentimental dreaming is its subject. The interconnections that we have noted between the female characters, including the mother, are such that the theme of desire takes on a 'universal' quality, and what is most consistent in the novel's presentation of sexuality in general is the fact that the object of desire is in all cases *absent*. For this reason alone, it seems legitimate to look at how the phenomenon of desire is described by psychoanalytical theorists:

> Le désir naît de l'écart entre le besoin et la demande; il est irréducible au besoin, car il n'est pas dans son principe relation à un objet réel, indépendant du sujet, mais au fantasme; il est irréductible à la demande, en tant qu'il cherche à s'imposer sans tenir compte du langage et de l'inconscient de l'autre, et exige d'être reconnu absolument par lui. (*11*, p.222)

It will be seen from this definition that 'le désir', when used by psychoanalysts, has a wider range of meanings than just sexual desire, and that the concept involves recognition by 'the other' ('l'autre', in psychoanalytical theory, as in existential psychology, has an almost absolute value, is unattainable by definition). This attempt at recognition, moreover, passes through *language*. It is partly on the basis of such a conception of 'le désir' that the theorists of *écriture* have described the modern text as a space of disguised and deferred meanings. These operate by means of two basic linguistic mechanisms: metaphor and metonymy.

A metaphor, in so far as it is a figure of speech which involves the *suppression* of the word or phrase literally designating the object or idea to be described, and the *replacement* of that word or phrase by others, on the basis of some analogy between the referents, is similar to what Freud called 'condensation', a regular process in dreams, in which repressed desires surface in disguise, concealed by words or images which are full of concealed meanings. Metonymy, on the other hand, is a figure of speech in which a word acquires its meanings from some instrumental, circumstantial, or cause-and-effect relationship with its context: 'the crown' can mean not just the physical object, but the person of the monarch, or the institution of monarchy, or monarchic authority. Metonymy has been linked, by modern literary theorists, to Freud's concept of 'displacement', the other regular device encountered in dream-work, whereby meanings and representations slide along associative chains towards images, particularly visualisable images, in which their latent content can be discharged (see *10*, p.507). Such images are characterised by their sensorial intensity. Displacement, in addition, is the most common form of censure mechanisms in dreams — what is repressed at one point will surface elsewhere, at another 'carrefour'. The death-chamber scene which we examined earlier (chapter 5) literally designates this process. *Histoire*, in which networks of metaphors (such as the knife image used to describe the mother's face) defy literal meanings, and quit the unified sites that are required by realism, is clearly open to interpretative readings which point to censorship, symbolic meanings and a sub-stratum of regressive desires, and if we look at love and desire in the novel in this spirit (a full interpretative analysis is impossible here) we quickly observe that much of what the psychoanalytical approach presupposes is evidenced by the text. According to psychoanalysis, the mother is of course the first object of the infant's love, since she provides the immediate satisfaction of basic needs. At a later stage, however, when the infant (infans = 'without speech') enters the symbolic world of language, the child has to learn how to defer its demands, and submit to a pre-existent order determined by a patriarchal family structure.

Just as the original fusion with the mother becomes the unattainable object of erotic impulses in the child, and later the adult, so, in its symbolic expression — in Romantic literature for example — love becomes an ideal, an abstract concept, as often as not inextricably linked to suffering and death.

The theory of the unconscious, however, entails recognising that all the contradictory and even perverse characteristics of infantile and childish love, from need, through demand, to 'le désir', remain intact, and clamour for satisfaction. In Freud's words, the unconscious is 'timeless'. Memory, on the other hand, mediates between the 'timeless' unconscious, and the mortal ongoing present. Conscious memory erects 'screens' or false memories which idealise and simplify childhood, and pro tect the psyche from potentially damaging repressed material. In dreams in particular, but also in creative work, perhaps particularly in creative work on *language*, where controls are partially lifted, some of these screens are dissolved and fragmented, and traces of early memories re-emerge, usually disguised, by the mechanisms of condensation and displacement. The ultimate source of many such memory traces can frequently be the anguish of separation from the mother that is the pre-condition for the recognition of the 'self'. In Lacan's theory of the 'mirror phase' (see *10*, pp.93-101), this emergent 'self' is in fact an imaginary construct — the self is viewed as 'other', as though duplicated in a mirror image. The 'self' or 'ideal ego' towards which we strive is thus, according to Lacan, a myth, forever denied realisation by the symbolic nature of our modes of thought and expression. In works of fiction, clearly, in so far as both narrators and characters remain authorial doubles, this situation expresses itself in the quest for 'the other' — the imaginary replica of the self, whose paradoxical existence/absence is made apparent only in language (see *10*, p.524). We shall see how this can apply to the shifts of identity which occur in section X of *Histoire* in my last chapter.

Returning to the themes of love and desire in the novel, we are now in a position to answer the question why it is that scenes involving the mother come at the beginning and the end of the text, and why some of the words connected with her (such as 'roses') and in particular the colour 'red' find their way into scenes involving both Corinne and Hélène, via images of flowers, of fruit, and of blood. These displacements correspond closely to what Freud describes in *The Interpretation of Dreams*, and can be related to what Gérard Genette has shown to be an interpenetration of the two linguistic figures of metaphor and metonymy (*5*, pp.41-63), in which the *comparant* in the metaphor (the image which takes the place of the *comparé*, or object described — such as 'lion' for 'brave man'), derives from both the immediate linguistic context, and from more distant sites, and carries with it symbolic meanings linked to repressed or censured material.

Both dreams and memories involve making present what is

absent, and are psychologically necessary in maintaining a sense of selfhood in relation to the past. Behind the sense of a 'self' is however, according to Lacan, an experience of loss: his theory of the 'mirror phase' entails a trauma of separation which, it has been claimed, may underly all acts of remembrance:

> Peut-être y a-t-il quelque paradoxe à soutenir que l'amour maternel puisse être traumatique. Mais c'est pourtant lui qui trace sur la passivité originaire les premiers moments de la mémoire.[11]

Perhaps then, this is why *Histoire*, 'roman de la mémoire', begins and ends with images of the mother, and returns finally to the ideal but unimaginable harmony of mother and foetus — the self *enclosed*, outside time, not yet tormented by memories of the past. Perhaps this is also why the early death of the narrator's mother is linked by displaced images (for example, the rose garland in the carpets in the background of the photograph of Van Velden's studio, which recall the mother's death-chamber (pp.16-20)) to guilt feelings connected with adult sexual relationships, and why Corinne intrudes upon memories of Hélène (pp.131-32) — because with the increasing liberty granted to the writing, there can be a *regression*, back to the primary source of desire, as a remarkable passage, at the end of section V clearly shows:

> rappelant ces réclames Pilules Orientales ou Kala Busta (avec ce B majuscule au double renflement opulent ...) que je pouvais voir dans les pages de publicité de la Mode Pratique parmi d'autre naïves et minutieusement dessinées par exemple celle pour une bouillie lactée représentant une gigantesque soupière à l'assaut de laquelle montait une nuée d'enfants liliputiens s'aidant d'échelles, une petite fille ... goûtant, espiègle, le contenu de la cuiller qu'elle avait réussi à tremper dans la bouillie
> entraînée par le poids tomberait basculerait en avant et

[11] René Laloue, 'Les écluses de la mémoire', *Revue Française de Psychanalyse*, 4, tome XLIII, juillet-août 1979, pp.746-47.

m'ensevelirait m'étoufferait sous la masse molle informe et
insexuée de sa poitrine maternelle (pp.183-84)

Once again, the text designates the generative processes, the
'mécanismes internes de prolifération' (to use Roubichou's
phrase) which are at work, for the capital B in the advertisement
for a breast-developing product leads to a fantasy involving
maternal milk and a giant maternal profile, which echoes the
very shape of the letter B. The fantasy wishes that cannot be expressed in the immediate context of the mother's death chamber
are displaced, put in the new context of an amusing description
of old magazine advertisements, but call attention to themselves
by designating the material linguistic vehicle on which they depend.

It is noteworthy that the arousal of erotic feelings in the narrator as an adolescent is associated with reading and translation.
He finds in Charles's library a copy of *The Golden Ass*, the
erotic fable by the classical author Apuleius, and searches in a
Latin dictionary for the translation of the difficult words. At
these points the narrator's sexual memories or fantasies take
over, and some powerfully erotic writing is produced. Already,
early on in the novel, postcards written in Spanish had had a
similar effect — the foreign language emphasising the opacity
and the physical characteristics of the words:

ces autres missives empreintes ou plutôt parfumées de la
lourde sensualité qui semble émaner de cette langue des
noms des mots eux-mêmes avec leur consonances lascives
et brutales leur senteur poivrée d'œillet et d'encens mêlés
les exhalaisons langoureuses et un peu moites des chairs
virginales des blancheurs des virginales sauvages noires et
secrètes toisons (p.35)

The quotations from *The Golden Ass* are mostly to be found
in section IV of *Histoire* (pp.109-47), where memories of a visit
to Greece with his wife Hélène, shortly after their marriage,
return to the narrator as he leaves the bank at midday and makes
his way to a restaurant. There was a quarrel, the cause of which

is not explained, and the narrator remembers trying unsuccessfully to repair the damage caused to their relationship, while they go through the motions of looking at the exhibits of a museum. These memories alternate with descriptions of postcards depicting battlefield scenes, such as the cratered landscapes of the first world war, where the father met his death. There are explicit connections between the guilt feelings aroused by these images, and the reading of the erotic text:

> une sorte de fascination vaguement honteuse, vaguement coupable, comme si elles détenaient la réponse à quelque secret capital du même ordre que celui des mots crus et anatomiques cherchés en cachette dans le dictionnaire, les lectures défendues, clandestines et décevantes (pp.116-17)

Descriptions of photographs taken during the Russian revolution in 1917, and quoted extracts from John Reed's eye-witness account *Ten Days that Shook the World* now alternate with lists of Latin words from *The Golden Ass*, as the act of translation arouses the adolescent. The intensity of this focus upon individual words is increased by the stress laid upon their materiality, by means of comparisons that are derived from the context of the museum, which remains throughout as a kind of first frame of reminiscence:

> les mots semblables à ces coupes, ces peignes, ces aiguilles, ces bracelets de bronze ou de cuivre verdis, un peu rongés, mais au contours précis, ciselés, que l'on peut voir dans les vitrines de ces musées (p.120)

A passage describing Hélène (her name means of course 'Greece') shows how complete the breakdown in communication with the narrator has become, and seems to anticipate her tragic death:

> son dos comme un mur énigmatique enfermant cachant cette espèce de tragique mélancolie cette chose sombre noire qui était déjà en elle comme un noyau de mort cachée

comme un poison un poignard sous le léger tissu de sa robe imprimée décorée de fleurs et plus profond sous sa chair ses seins doux que j'aimais presser contre mes tempes avec leurs bouts pâles fragiles)

prêts à tomber (les mots), aurait-on dit, en une poussière de particules friables brunâtres de rouille qui semblait s'échapper des pages du dictionnaire en même temps qu'un impalpable et subtil relent de cendres (pp.120-21)

A reference to a scene reminiscent of the aftermath of a volcanic eruption heightens further the associations between sexual excitement and cataclysmic violence:

le doigt, l'ongle immobilisé sous le mot en caractères gras: nervus, tendon, ligament, membre viril, nerf, rigoris nimietate rumpatur, sur le point d'éclater, bourgeon, tendu à se rompre ... (p.121)

After a return to the present, and the narrator's wish to avoid meeting again the old man who had reminded him of Hélène and her death, the museum scene again returns, but the fictional past has dissolved, and the text gives way to scriptural effects in the present of the writing/reading processes. This occurs with the description of carved inscriptions and statuary, with a play on the words *lézard* and *lézarde* (p.129). A lizard appears out of a crack in a statue, then disappears back into 'la fente aux bords dentelés qui coupe en deux les rangées de lettres' (p.129). The lizard materialises out of the inscribed letters, and vanishes back into them — what more explicit exhibition could we require of the materiality of the word, and the imaginary status of the referent (or, more precisely the referents, since only the presence or absence of the final [d] sound determines the two meanings 'crack' and 'lizard')? Only a page later the text reminds us of the fragility of lizards' tails — it is as if what we have just observed were being confirmed: if you break off the final [d] of *lézarde* you obtain [lezar]. The lizard comes out of, and disappears back into the inscribed letters of the text of the novel, which has, in addition, illustrated the 'fente', the gap between the material presence of the word and the purely mental image it refers to. What is more, the edges of the openings are 'dentelés' — the description includes, metaphorically, the mouth, the organ of speech production (sexual connotations are equally evident, in the form of a latent castration phobia, in which the female genitals constitute a threat to the male). Speech, however, is evanescent, whereas writing (inscription) acquires a solidity subject only to the physical decomposition of the paper (or stone) — as is indicated in the passage quoted earlier ('prêts à tomber (les mots), aurait-on dit, en une poussière de particules friables,' etc.).

Two pages later, a further description of the lizard confirms its demonstrative function in the text, for with its body it writes the letter S:

> cette fois il se tordait vers le bas dessinant un S horizontal mouvant très vite ses petites pattes griffues puis changea brusquement de direction et remontant toute la surface de la dalle traversa l'inscription en oblique disparut au-delà du bord supérieur (pp.133-34)

Not only produced by the writing, the lizard thus becomes a symbolic producer of writing: the referents (fictional objects like the lizard) are now on the point of being free to take over the writing of the text, of usurping the narrator's traditional role. We shall see in the next chapter how close *Histoire* gets to this stage, particularly in section IX.

A scene that we have already mentioned now returns: Charles contemplates a freshly filled grave, noticing in the earth mound tiny fossil shells and little blades of grass beginning to grow. The cemetery is near an aerodrome, and an aeroplane swoops low overhead. This recurrent scene in *Histoire* is a re-writing of one that first appeared in *La Corde raide* (1947), but which is equally enigmatic — it is a kind of textual dead-end — whatever the 'story' is or was about comes to an end there. The scene, when it first appears, is linked only to Charles:

... son nom même pas encore gravé sur une dalle, et lui, lui
qui ne pouvait que perdre les femmes se tenant là, devant
cette tombe fraîche (p.132)

The source of what the narrator imagines is a postcard, the text
of which gives Charles's own description of the grave (p.145).
When fragments of this, or a similar scene, reappear, it is after
the switches of identity that occur in section X.

Returning to the sequence of passages which lead to the erotic
centre of the novel, there is another 'intertextual' reference, this
time to an ancestor of de Reixach. As we saw, the name de
Reixach, via the nick-name 'Baronne Cerise', evokes childhood
memories of cherry-picking, with Corinne and Paulou. The
transition from the scene in the Greek museum, to the memories
involving Corinne occurs, unusually, *within* a paragraph block,
and in such a way that the switch of context can cause some initial confusion:

faisant semblant de s'intéresser aux inscriptions rédigées en
grec
     Hélène arrétons veux-tu?
     elle ne bougea pas toujours penchée en avant dans sa
robe couleur de fruits de feuillages. Les branches
remuèrent je pouvais voir ses jambes nues mais pas le reste
du corps disparaissant dans les feuilles agitées de brèves
secousses Elle s'était écorchée en grimpant Un mince filet
de sang descendait le long de son mollet (p.134)

When the grandmother calls out Corinne's name, any remaining doubts disappear, but a few lines later, there is another
abrupt transition, this time to a more specifically erotic memory
involving Corinne as a girl:

Elle en avait mis des doubles comme des boucles d'oreilles
... Corinne aux boucles d'oreille corail ... El les détacha de
son oreille ses cheveux étaient dénoués emmêlés crinibus-
que dissolutis paulisper etiam glabellum feminal rosea
palmula potius obumbrans de industria quam tegens

> verecundia ombrageant dissimulant mal (plus par coquet-
> terie que par pudeur — épilé, glabre) la rose, la mince ligne
> l'étroite fente couleur de pétale rosea placé entre feminal et
> palmula comme une unique source de couleur (pp.134-35)

Although the fictional pretext for this scene — Corinne's shav-
ing of her pubic hair — locates it in the narrator's youth, the
context of scenes describing Hélène leads to a near breakdown
of separate identities: the erotic text, in particular the Latin
words, so concentrates the suppressed or censored memories
that, in the end the writing produces a purely *linguistic* fantasy
(quite literally):

> je la pris dans mes bras ma langue dans sa bouche puis
> descendis le long de son cou ses seins son ventre enfonçai
> ma langue dedans glabellum était-ce en me rappelant ce
> passage que je lui avais demandé de le faire (p.135)

In these passages, it is clear that the erotic element is doubled by
an entirely implicit commentary upon words, and the power of
attraction that they exert, as the desire that they seek to describe
slides away along associative chains. In the word 'rosea', for example, 'placé entre feminal et palmula comme une unique
source de couleur', we have the unifying seme (unit of meaning)
which links all the female characters to the narrator, and which
thus shows, as psychoanalysis claims, how all sexual desire, once
the false screens of 'memory' are lifted, bears traces of its maternal source. The word 'rosea' glows 'comme une unique source
de couleur' not just because of the immediate sexual connotations, but because it gathers in to itself the bouquets of roses in
the mother's room, the rose pattern in the carpet, the roses on
the priest's vestment, memories of Hélène, the childhood
episodes with Corinne, and reveals itself finally to be no more
than a word.

As in some previous examples, the letters of the text now
assert their materiality, their primary status as graphic signs:

haec simul dicens insenso grabulato escaladant le lit elle
aCCourt aile de ses cheveux défaits figure volante les deux
boucles jumelles de l'*l* double alanguies inclinées par la
course les deux C semblables à deux dos ou plutôt au même
dos répété deux fois comme les contours d'un personnage
sur une photo bougée forme fuligineuse d'un corps ou
plutôt d'un mouvement une jambe levée semblable à quelque figure volante écartelée sa fente la moule ce coquillage
au goût de sel entrouvert d'un trait de crayon rapide par la
position de la cuisse ouverte contre laquelle la ligne
sinueuse de son ventre son flanc son sein vient s'écraser on-
doyer criant de joie s'abattant s'ébattant ... (pp.135-36)

The description has now become an example of 'self-
representation', as the 'memory' (I called these erotic scenes
'fantasies' a moment ago, but this is equally misleading) is
transformed into a drawing — the 'fente', or object of desire at
the level of fantasy, is 'entrouvert d'un trait de crayon rapide': it
is revealed as a representation of a representation.

7. Writing and Representation

In sections IX and X of *Histoire* (pp.288-346) all the questions, conflicts and ambiguities that have been discussed in this volume come to a head. Section IX is arguably the most unified and coherent chapter in the novel, consisting entirely of a description of a photograph that the narrator has come across among the postcards, in which Charles is seen sitting in the painter Van Velden's studio, together with an unidentified 'homme barbu', the painter himself, and a naked female model.

The photograph is singled out as important by a parenthesis which can be read as designating its function as an essential thematic motif, a pretext for authorial commentary, and also, ultimately, an emblem of the central enigma of *Histoire*:

> et pas une carte postale cette fois, mais une photographie (et venue là comment? parmi les vues de déserts, de forêts tropicales, de cathédrales milanaises, de montagnes enneigées et de paquebots appareillant) (p.288)

Charles is shown to be playing a role equivalent to that of a satirical double for the writer, embodying the artistic myths which, in our culture, have allowed artists in all fields to pose as exceptional beings. This role is indicated in the narrator's memories of how, as a boy, he imagined Charles in the company of writers and artists in Paris:

> personnage vaguement mythique sous l'aspect duquel ... je l'avais imaginé ou plutôt ce double en quelque sorte exotique, anachronique ... dont, dans mon esprit d'enfant, il devait prendre la forme lorsqu'il nous quittait, avec la coiffure romantique, le gilet romantique, le pantalon mastic, le porte-fusain-scalpel, au milieu du décor romantique et sévère composé par le chevalet, le compas et la main de plâtre sectionnée au poignet suspendue derrière lui (p.288)

The photograph begins by demolishing the 'romantic' aura
that the narrator's childish imagination had created — Charles is
unrecognisable; the familiar face is as unlike what he would have
expected as a field seen before and after it had been ploughed.
Now, Charles is merely a 'figurant' (p.289).

The photograph is blurred, as a result, the narrator surmises,
of it having been taken with a camera having an automatic shutter. Because of this, the figure of the painter ('peut-être ce Van
Velden' (p.289)) is seen in triple exposure:

> la partie droite de la photographie occupée au premier plan
> par l'image fuligineuse (non pas floue si l'on regarde plus
> attentivement, mais bougée) du Hollandais, ou plutôt par
> trois images du même visage (pp.289-90)

The description of the photograph now becomes a reconstruction of the events which preceded the moment when the
camera's shutter operated, before the painter had time to pose.
The blurring of the image creates a contrast between the images
on the left and centre of the photograph, which are frozen in
time:

> donnant l'illusion que la photographie est un de ces instan-
> tanés, une de ces coupes lamelliformes pratiquées à
> l'intérieur de la durée et où les personnages aplatis,
> enfermés dans les contours précis, sont pour ainsi dire
> artificiellement isolés de la série des attitudes qui précèdent
> et qui suivent (p.291)

and the triple silhouette of the painter:

> la trace fuligineuse laissée par le visage au cours de ses
> divers changements de positions restituant à l'événement
> son épaisseur, postulant ... la double suite des instants
> passés et futurs, la double série, dans le même cadrage et le
> même décor, des positions respectivement occupées par les
> divers personnages avant et après (p.291)

The reconstruction of this temporal series reveals immediately the fundamental problem of narration, that of postulating the *order* of events:

> Plus tard seulement ils (les autres personnages figurant sur la photo) étaient venus occuper leurs places. Mais comment? Suivant quel ordre? (p.294)

The alternatives are now becoming clear: representation depends either upon the artificial arresting of time (for something to be photographed, painted, or described it must stop moving), or upon a hazardous and arbitrary attempt to impose order, by the creation of a sequence which corresponds to the mind's demand for logical connections between the series of moments involved in any 'event'. When, a little later, the narrator imagines how the scene must have appeared from Charles's point of view another essential element in the demonstration emerges — the fact that the sequence (either of moments in an event, or of elements in a description) depends, for its reconstruction, upon the memory of the subject who is observing or narrating the scene. Charles, somewhat embarrassed, but also fascinated by the naked model, sees her obliquely:

> le corps nu placé par conséquent, par rapport à lui, dans cette zone marginale du champ visuel où les choses n'apparaissent plus que sous la forme de taches vagues, imprécises, de sorte que l'oeil non pas voit mais bien plutôt se souvient non de la fatidique succession (ou suite, ou énumération) de parties — chevelure, épaules, seins, hanches, ventre, cuisses, le vieux rideau drapé contre le mur en guise de fond et la couverture tunisienne — dans leur ordre monotone, mais d'une combinaison, d'un ombreux et fulgurant enchevêtrement de lumières et de lignes où les éléments éclatés, dissociés se regroupent selon le foisonnant et rigoureux désordre de la mémoire
>
> (pp.295-96)

Here, the text is commenting directly upon the formal basis of its own composition: the logical order of traditional narrative and description (which conforms to the same requirements, in spite of what Jean Ricardou has shown to be the inherent conflict with narration which it entails (see *14*, pp.30-31)), is subject to the 'rigoureux désordre' of memory. In other words, memory has become a function no longer determined by the demands of representation, but which imposes its own specific order upon the 'éléments éclatés', or the fragments of narration and description which constitute the text. This 'memory', cannot be identified with that of either author or narrator and is neither 'inside' nor 'outside' the fictional illusion, since this is itself in the process of being deconstructed. Only the concept of 'textual memory' can now account for what begins to occur openly in the writing.

Already, Charles's fascination with the naked model has allowed the writing to regress to what we described earlier as the source of both erotic and artistic desire, as the narrator imagines his initiation into adult sexuality, but in an extraordinary passage, following the last one quoted, where the 'éléments éclatés' are assembled into an abstract pattern of shapes and colours, any attempts to use memory as a basis for a reconstruction of reality is abandoned, and with it the obligation to use words as instruments, for naming the world. Language now becomes as much the subject of the writer's sensuous pleasure as the vehicle for more obscure impulses:

> l'esprit (ou plutôt: encore l'œil, mais plus seulement l'œil, et pas encore l'esprit: cette partie de notre cerveau où passe l'espèce de couture, le hâtif et grossier faufilage qui relie l'innommable au nommé) non pas disant mais sentant:
> (p.297)

The paragraph block which follows, and which was the subject of a short paper that I gave to the 1974 colloquium on Simon (*4*, pp.387-94) is unprecedented in the novel, and in Simon's work up until this point. In it, we can see words coming together according to processes that cannnot be accounted for, unless the hypotheses of 'textual memory', and the disappearance of the psychological subject, are accepted. The passage includes elements that can be traced back as far as *Le Tricheur*, and which are inscribed again in *La Bataille de Pharsale*, but above all it illustrates the return to what I earlier described as the erotic source of the scriptural energy of *Histoire*, the 'unique source de couleur' which radiates throughout the novel, counteracting the morbidity of so much of the fictional content:

> éventail de plis rassemblés par la tête du clou rouillé lourde queue d'étalon noir peignée parmi les ramages de roses éteintes, plage, amas confus nacre noir ivoire, coude dans la flasque mollesse de coussin olivé éclaboussé d'ombre vert pomme mais impossible de voir la peau légèrement rugueuse là rosie au milieu des langues d'herbe le pis de la chèvre pesant dans la paume exhalant l'odeur sucrée fade des orangers fleurs pour les mariages mince trait de métal doré au doigt jetant des éclats orange citron pacotille trouvée dans la sciure sous la tente rouge en plein vent baiser au lèvres cyclamen cachées aussi sous l'essaim de mouches lappant le lait répandu flaque au-dessus des bandes coloriées bigarrées (p.297)

While the passage purports, at one level, to describe the model as viewed by Charles, the words themselves are operating according to other principles, gathering together at this crucial point in the novel references that are scattered throughout the text (and, as I indicated just now, beyond it). Thus, the words 'noir peignée parmi les ramages les roses éteintes' recall the mother: 'sa chevelure dénouée répandue en éventail sur ses épaules et son dos un long peignoir traînant sur le tapis aux guirlandes de roses' (p.34). The transformation of 'peignoir' into 'noir peignée' shows us that our *lecture/réécriture* of the text can transgress the arbitrary limits we assign to poetic procedures in prose fiction, and examine words that are no longer self-contained lexical units; they are broken down, transformed by associations at the level of individual phonemes and graphemes (that is, units of sound, and also individual graphic symbols). Rhymes and assonance also bring together the 'éléments

éclatés': 'cl*ou* r*ou*illé l*ou*rde', 'n*oi*r iv*oi*re', '*p*is ... *p*esant dans la
*p*aume', 'f*l*asque mo*ll*esse de cou*ss*in o*l*ive é*cl*aboussé',
'*m*ariages *m*ince trait de *m*étal'. The story that cannot be told,
the absence at the heart of the novel, is again evoked, and in
such a way that both the narrator's desire, and the enigma of his
wife's death, are called up (by a displaced reference to the
graveside scene that we looked at earlier): 'impossible de voir ...
là rosie au milieu des langues d'herbe'. The tragic story of two
(?) failed marriages is then hinted at with the mention of the
model's ring, and again the writing confirms that the source of
its productivity is linguistic, as oral references are grouped
together in the final sequence: 'baiser aux lèvres cyclamen
cachées aussi sous l'essaim de mouches lappant le lait répandu'.
Liberated from representation, the language of the text can
assert its materiality, and can once again play the childish games
which are at the root of creativity[12]: the 'regression' that allows
the novel to escape from the obligation of telling a story is thus
transformed into its contrary, an artistically progressive move
towards a non-representational aesthetic of writing, and to a tru-
ly poetic encounter with language, all the more impressive for remaining faithful, however indirectly, to the lost object of its
desire, and thus to the universal basis of human feelings. Even at
the most abstract theoretical level, the conflict between representation and *écriture* does not erase an impression of intense
physical nostalgia. Claude Simon may dismiss the psychological
content of *Histoire* as 'scories', but for many readers it will remain a great novel largely because of the depth of feeling that
the text conveys, and the sensuousness of the language.

[12] See 'Creativity and its origins', in D.W. Winnicot's seminal work *Playing and
Reality*, Pelican Books, 1974, pp.76-100.

Conclusion — History and Story

In an interview published in *La Quinzaine Littéraire* (15-31 décembre, 1967) Claude Simon quoted a definition of the word 'histoire' that he had found in a dictionary:

> J'ai trouvé dans le Littré, parmi d'autres, cette acception du mot 'histoire': *Dans le langage familier, se dit pour un objet quelconque qu'on ne peut ou on ne veut pas nommer.*

His interviewer, Madeleine Chapsal, had asked him whether or not the novel was also 'l'histoire d'un mensonge', alluding in this way to the autobiographical hypothesis, and to another meaning of the word that Simon had not chosen to evoke. Simon's reply was somewhat evasive:

> Une chose, on la cache, on se la cache, on la découvre, on l'avait gommée ... Il se pose pour tout romancier une question troublante, qui parle?
> *M.C. Vous ne le savez pas?*
> C.S. Non. C'est difficile de décider, croyez-moi ... Mon narrateur, c'est apparement le neveu. Mais en parlant de son oncle, il dit tout à coup 'je' au lieu de 'il'. Est-ce parce qu'il s'identifie à son oncle à force d'imaginer ce que celui-ci a vécu? Est-ce au contraire parce qu'en réalité il prête à son oncle une histoire qui lui est arrivée à lui et que l'oubliant il se coupe ... ou peut-être le narrateur est-il l'oncle qui s'invente un neveu en cherchant à imaginer comment celui-ci pourrait le voir, lui ...

By throwing back the question in this way, Simon was clearly poking fun, in a fairly gentle way, at the 'realist' assumption behind it, but when I questioned him further on this point, in a conversation in his flat in Paris in 1971, he confirmed that while he was writing section X of the novel, he found that the substitution of identities had occurred without him having taken any conscious decision to that effect — he did not know, from that point on in the text, who his narrator was. The only possible conclusion was that the writing itself had 'taken over', and was producing effects which were unexpected. Instead of attempting to resolve the problem, he allowed the process to continue, until his only guide, in composing the last sections of the novel, which are increasingly fragmented, was a system of colour coding, in which he used coloured pens to identify and organise the sequence of paragraph blocks, according to largely intuitive associations between colours.

These remarks, however anecdotal they may be, show how far the novel eventually takes us from the story ('qu'on ne peut ou ne veut pas nommer'), a tragic episode in the writer's life which is transformed and transcended, until it becomes an emblem for all such untellable stories, and for the basic fact that readers in particular tend to deny: that life cannot be lived again, or recovered, or recreated, in fiction. The suppression of the autobiographical source of *Histoire* is thus not a dishonest evasion by the writer — it is evidence, rather, of exceptional artistic integrity, and of a desire to wean the novels away from personal experience into new areas of discovery, as Simon's remarks on the genesis of the subsequent novel, *La Bataille de Pharsale* show:

> J'étais encore en train de travailler *Histoire* quand je suis allé en Grèce ... en grec ancien le mot *istoria* ne signifie pas 'histoire' dans le sens où nous l'entendons aujourd'hui, mais *recherche, enquête*. C'est cela qui m'intéresse, cette recherche de ce que l'écriture va m'apporter. (*8*, p.189)

This is the quest which gradually takes over in *Histoire*, as the formal problems created by the proliferation of the text begin to transcend the original autobiographical pretext. The novel thus becomes the story of an artistic revolution in process, and tells both of what must be abandoned in terms of conventional expectations (on the part of writer *and* reader), and of what can be gained, in terms of creative freedom, and the open future of the text to come, as opposed to the closed worlds of the past, and of realist fiction. *Histoire* tells a universally familiar (and familial) story of death, of loss, and of desire, but it is also an incomparable encounter with language. A short study such as this can do no more than begin to explore some of the pathways through the novel that open up at each of the 'carrefours' in the text, each word of which is potentially another 'nœud de significations'.[13] Only specific acts of reading can continue the process.

---

[13] Simon (quoting Lacan), in 'La fiction mot à mot', *4*, pp.73-97.

Bibliography

A. *MAJOR WORKS BY CLAUDE SIMON*
(Place of publication is Paris, and the publisher Les Editions de Minuit unless otherwise stated.)
Le Tricheur, Editions du Sagittaire, 1945
La Corde raide, Editions du Sagittaire, 1947
Gulliver, Calmann-Lévy, 1952
Le Sacre du printemps, Calmann-Lévy, 1954
Le Vent: Tentative de restitution d'un retable baroque, 1957
L'Herbe, 1958
La Route des Flandres, 1960
Le Palace, 1962
Histoire, 1967
La Bataille de Pharsale, 1969
Orion aveugle, Geneva, Skira, 1970
Les Corps conducteurs, 1971
Triptyque, 1973
Leçon de choses, 1975
Les Géorgiques, 1981

B. *BOOKS AND ARTICLES REFERRED TO IN THIS VOLUME*
 1. Benveniste, Emile, *Problèmes de linguistique générale, I,* Paris, Gallimard, 1956
 2. Carroll, David, 'Diachrony and Synchrony in *Histoire*', *Modern Language Notes*, 92, no.4, May 1977, pp.797-824
 3. Colloque de Cerisy, *Nouveau roman: hier, aujourd'hui*, Vol.2, 'Pratiques', Paris, Union Générale d'Editions, 1972
 4. Colloque de Cerisy, *Claude Simon: analyse, théorie*, Paris, Union Générale d'Editions, 1975
 5. Genette, Gérard, *Figures III*, Paris, Editions du Seuil, 1972
 6. Heath, Stephen, *The Nouveau Roman*, London, Elek, 1972
 7. Jiménez-Fajardo, Salvador, *Claude Simon*, Boston, G.K. Hall & Co., 1975
 8. Knapp, Bettina L., 'Interview avec Claude Simon', *Kentucky Romance Quarterly*, XVI, 2 (1969), pp.182-89
 9. Loubère, J.A.E., *The Novels of Claude Simon*, Ithaca and London, Cornell University Press, 1965
 10. Lacan, Jacques, *Ecrits*, Paris, Editions du Seuil, 1966
 11. Laplanche, J., et J.-B. Pontalis, *Vocabulaire de la Psychanalyse*, Paris, Presses Universitaires de France, 1967

12. Pugh, Anthony Cheal, 'Du *Tricheur* à *Triptyque*, et inversement', *Etudes Littéraires* (Laval), Vol.9, no.1, avril 1976, pp.137-60

13. Ricardou, Jean, *Problèmes du nouveau roman*, Paris, Editions du Seuil, 1967

14. ——, *Le Nouveau Roman*, Paris, Editions du Seuil, 1973

15. Roubichou, Gérard, *Lecture de 'l'Herbe' de Claude Simon*, Lausanne, L'Age d'Homme, 1976

16. ——, 'Continu et discontinu ou l'hérétique alinéa (Notes sur la lecture d'*Histoire*)', *Etudes Littéraires* (Laval), Vol.9, no.1, avril 1976, pp.125-36

17. Sykes, Stuart, *Les Romans de Claude Simon*, Paris, Editions de Minuit, 1979